Why is Jesus a **pocket GIANT**?

Because he founded the largest religion in the world.

Because he he is regarded as 'the most important person in history' (Time Magazine).

Because 2.2 billion Christians today view him as the saviour of the world.

Because he connects three world religions, representing half the world's population.

DR EDWARD KESSLER MBE is a leading thinker in interfaith relations, primarily between Jews, Christians and Muslims. He is Founder Director of the Woolf Institute and Fellow of St Edmund's College, Cambridge.

JESUS

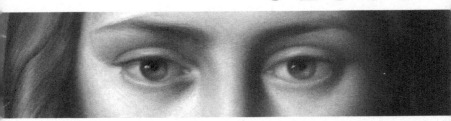

POCKET
GIANTS

ED
KESSLER

Cover image: Shutterstock

First published 2016

The History Press
The Mill, Brimscombe Port
Stroud, Gloucestershire, GL5 2QG
www.thehistorypress.co.uk

© Ed Kessler, 2016

The right of Ed Kessler to be identified as the Author
of this work has been asserted in accordance with the
Copyright, Designs and Patents Act 1988.

British Library Cataloguing in Publication Data.
A catalogue record for this book is available from the British Library.

ISBN 978 0 7509 61240

Typesetting and origination by The History Press
Printed and bound by TJ International Ltd, Padstow, Cornwall.

Contents

Introduction

It may surprise the reader that we know very little about a man who was ranked by *Time* magazine and *Wikipedia* as the most important historical figure of all time and who also topped the list of Google searches for the most well known person in history. (Interestingly, in the Google top ten were three other biblical figures: Abraham [third], Moses [fourth] and Paul [fifth].) Yet, the religion named after Jesus fills an immense place in human history, and civilisation itself is unintelligible without an understanding of Christianity and Jesus Christ.

In today's interconnected world, we are not only surrounded by Christian civilisation and culture but we breathe it in; it is part of us all – Christian and non-Christian, religious and secular, young and old.

This, it seems to me, refutes the criticism, which dominated Western thinking only a couple of decades ago: religion was a fading entity and secularism would soon push it to the margins and eventually to extinction. This theory of modernisation, based on the theories of Marx, Durkheim and Weber, proposed that as societies modernise they irrevocably grow more secular. Recent history has shown otherwise. Religion is a major driving force in contemporary society and in the words of the American sociologist Peter Berger, 'the world is as furiously religious as it ever was, and in some places more so than ever'.

According to the 2013 Pew Survey, 85 per cent of the global population belong to a specific religion, the largest of which is Christianity (2.2 billion). Although in some countries such as the UK, an increasing proportion do not identify themselves as religious (25 per cent according to the 2011 census) the world as a whole is witnessing a notable resurgence of religion's influence including a dramatic expansion of Christianity in China (even though it is officially an atheist state) and new forms of Christianity, such as Pentecostal and Evangelical Christianity which is now the second largest Christian denomination, (estimated at 500 million), after Roman Catholics at 1.2 billion.

Before we begin this exploration of Jesus and explain how he changed the world, I would like to make a confession. Even though there are many scholars who have devoted their life to the study of Jesus and the New Testament, I am not one; nor am I a Christian.

What are the advantages and disadvantages for such a person to write this book? To be an outsider should, in theory, make one impartial but I think it is inconceivable to write an impartial study of Jesus, even if the author is an atheist. Would this book be better, if written by a detached author, without Christian beliefs? Whilst there are advantages to such a position there are also disadvantages. Outsiders too have their own presuppositions, which may make them, unconsciously or not, prejudiced one way or another. Indeed, the outsider may be unable to fully understand a religion or do it justice.

Having engaged in inter-religious conversation and study for more than thirty years, I am aware that one can only truly know a religion from within. Its intimacy does not reveal itself to outsiders, at least not easily. Study is insufficient; one needs familiarity. The secrets of a religion are not simply learned from its literature – they are discovered by encountering its adherents, listening to the stories they tell, reflecting on the art they produce, the deeds they do and spending time in the buildings in which they worship.

At the same time, of course, there are obvious disadvantages from writing within, not least the lack of impartiality. Living within a Christian faith may make the writer blind to reasonable criticism and reluctant to acknowledge incoherence or inconsistency. Perhaps no adequate account can ever be written; if you are within you cannot be impartial; if you are without you cannot know.

Both advantages and disadvantages are increased when a Jew writes about Jesus. I am familiar with the environment in which Jesus lived and taught. His thought is not so 'other'. I stand outside the sanctuary of Christianity but live and teach so much among those within that I can appreciate their feelings and their sensibilities. During my teaching career, at least a third of my students have taken positions of leadership in the church and from them (and my Christian colleagues) I have learned, and continue to learn, a great deal. I am familiar with the New Testament accounts of Jesus because in a certain sense, the New Testament is a collection of Jewish writings, much of which was written by Jews; all of it about a Jew. In sum, I claim Jesus as one of my own.

But, the very fact Judaism and Christianity have so much in common and are so closely related makes this book no less challenging to write. Indeed, just where some of the intimacies begin so the two religions differ. The Cross of Christ is indeed a stumbling block for Jews – no less a stumbling block than the Torah for Christians.

The challenge is made more demanding because this book is about a person upon whom is based the religion that has an intimate yet traumatic relationship with my own. I write about the person after whom Christianity was named, which has often claimed to have superseded Judaism and has persecuted my forebears. Yet, the same religion has also rediscovered a close relationship with its 'elder sibling', expressing both admiration and desire for reconciliation. Among Jews themselves there has also been a rapprochement, epitomised by the comment of Jewish philosopher, Martin Buber, who called Jesus his 'elder brother' and also by the publication of *Dabru Emet* (*Speak Truth*) in 2000, a document comprising the most positive affirmation of Christianity ever written, signed by over 200 rabbis and other Jewish leaders.

For those readers who start this book with a healthy dose of doubt and cynicism about whether we can know anything about the historical Jesus, in the spirit of Buber

I suggest the historicity does not, from one point of view, matter. It is not a question of true or false. There are degrees of historicity, and even kinds, of truth. (As Niels Bohr once said, 'there are trivial truths and there are great truths. The opposite of a trivial truth is plainly false. The opposite of a great truth is also true.') What intrigues me about Jesus is the meaning of his teachings rather than Christology, the stories taught by and about Jesus rather than the theology itself. In other words, I focus on the narrative not only on what Jesus told his disciples but what that tells us today about what John Templeton called the 'Big Questions': who we are, where we came from, what is our place in the universe and what, therefore, we are called on to do.

One reason why Jesus and his followers changed the world is because the narratives about Jesus contained multiple points of view. There are many sides to Jesus. He is open to more than one interpretation and more than one level of interpretation. The stories Jesus told enabled Christians to offer the world a multitude of meanings and interpretations. For 2,000 years, the world has received these stories with an outstretched arm.

At the same time, however, one common theme running alongside these multiple meanings has been a strong, sometimes violent, desire among Christians to search for the single 'true' Jesus, often in conflict with other Christians (as well as followers of other religions). Should Christians encounter Jesus more in the pages of scripture (Protestant) than through mass (Catholic)? I suspect that

Jesus himself would suggest that the truth of one does not entail the falsity of others – indeed the very words 'true' and 'false' seem out of place. Unfortunately, until recently, the desire to discover the 'true' Jesus has resulted in a narrative of displacement – of fellow Christians as well as Jews, Muslims and other non-Christians.

The first half of this book focuses on the narratives about Jesus, his teachings and his life, for it is the teaching that abides and the imitation of his life by his countless followers that have changed the world. Chapter 1 explores his life, from birth to death. Whilst there is a limited amount we know about historical Jesus I provide a general outline of what we do know, focusing on his brief ministry in Galilee, which lasted between one and three years, before concluding with the pilgrimage to Jerusalem, controversial action at the Temple, trial(s) and eventually, crucifixion by Roman imperial decree.

Chapter 2 reflects on the most important teachings of Jesus. It begins with a discussion of his use of parables and ways of teaching, including an often-overlooked feature of his ministry – his use of humour. Much of the rest of this chapter examines what Jesus meant by announcing the 'Kingdom of God', his most well known teaching, which is closely associated with his call for repentance.

In the second half of the book I focus on the development of Christianity, from the experience of Jesus by his followers soon after his death to the modern day. Chapter 3 describes the growth of Christianity and why it not only survived the death of Jesus but also flourished.

I consider both the continued Jewish practice by the Jewish followers of Jesus, as well as the incredible success of the mission to the Gentiles, initiated by the apostle Paul. Within a few centuries Christianity became the official religion of the Roman Empire under Constantine, not only becoming a global religion but also the largest of all.

Chapter 4 explores views of Jesus from beyond Christianity, beginning with the religion of Jesus, Judaism, before considering its 'sister' religion Islam, which contains many similar teachings about Jesus in its own Scriptures. The Eastern religions, Hinduism and Buddhism, also have a number of similarities and differences with the teachings of Jesus and the chapter concludes with the influence of Jesus in unexpected places – Communism, which is normally associated with atheism, and capitalism which for some prioritises the worship of Mammon above the divine.

I hope this book helps readers, whether Christian or not, to understand how Jesus changed the world: humans can be one thing or another but Jesus can be more. It is the diverse applicability of his teachings, as well as the malleability of the figure of Jesus, that enables me to claim him as the person who changed the world more than any other.

And is there another way to justify such a claim? Simply this: there are more followers of Jesus than any other religion (or secular ideology) in the world.

1

The Historical Jesus

A Brief Biography

Jesus was born around 4 BCE although none of the gospels shows much interest in dating his birth. The Gospel of Matthew simply states that his birth occurred 'in the days of Herod the king'. He grew up in Nazareth, located in Galilee, in the land of Israel. We know very little of Jesus' childhood, although numerous legends and stories came to be associated with him, which explain that he was descended from King David, possessed similar attributes to numerous biblical figures and had a filial relation to God through the power of the Holy Spirit.

His early life is referred to as the 'unknown years' and the famous infancy narratives inform us more about Christian theology than historical memory, echoing biblical stories, such as the visits of the angel to Hagar (Genesis 16:7–14) and post-biblical accounts such as Miriam's dream of the miraculous birth of her brother, Moses (Pseudo-Philo).

According to the Gospel of Luke, Mary encounters the angel Gabriel, who announces that although she is a virgin, she will conceive by the work of the Holy Spirit:

[26] In the sixth month the angel Gabriel was sent by God to a town in Galilee called Nazareth, [27] to a virgin engaged to a man whose name was Joseph, of the house of David. The virgin's name was Mary. [28] And he came to her and said, 'Greetings, favoured one! The Lord is with you.' [29] But she was much perplexed by his words and pondered what sort of greeting this might be. [30] The angel said to her, 'Do not be afraid, Mary, for you have found favour with God. [31] And now, you will conceive in your womb and bear a son, and you will name him Jesus. [32] He will be great, and will be called the Son of the Most High, and the Lord God will give to him the throne of his ancestor David. [33] He will reign over the house of Jacob forever, and of his kingdom there will be no end.' [34] Mary said to the angel, 'How can this be, since I am a virgin?' [35] The angel said to her, 'The Holy Spirit will come upon you, and the power of the Most High will overshadow you; therefore the child to be born will be holy; he will be called Son of God.' (Luke 1:26–35)

The Jewish context pervades the Gospel accounts. Luke, for example, describes Jesus as a precocious 12-year-old engaging in a debate with adults in the Jerusalem Temple (2:39–52). Jesus was brought up in a traditional Jewish household and his family would have been observant of the Jewish commandments: paid tithes, kept the Sabbath, circumcised their males, attended synagogue, observed purity laws in relation to childbirth and menstruation, kept the dietary code and so on.

While the Gospels record disputes about Jesus' interpretation of a few of these, the notion of a Christian Jesus, who did not live by Jewish law and culture, or at least by its ethical values, does not fit historical reality. Unlike some of his contemporaries, such as Philip and Andrew, Jesus bore a Jewish name: Yeshua. His brothers are named James (Jacob), Joseph (Josef), Judas or Jude (Judah), Simon (Simeon), and his father, Joseph and mother, Mary (Miriam).

Jesus never travelled outside of the Middle East and never married. There is no evidence of sexual relations, still less of any children. The idea of a secret bloodline may have been the exciting premise of the *Da Vinci Code*, Dan Brown's 2003 best-selling thriller, but like the Hollywood blockbuster, the book is based on fantasy, not fact.

Like the Buddha and Socrates (and other great teachers of the ancient world), Jesus wrote nothing about himself as far as we know and the New Testament sources are complex and multi-layered. If the first couple of decades of Jesus' life are almost a complete mystery, he came to public attention in the late 20s of the first century CE, when he was about 30 years old. For Mark, which most scholars believe to be the earliest of the Gospels, the Jesus story begins with his baptism as an adult, with no hint of a special circumstance at his birth:

[9] In those days Jesus came from Nazareth of Galilee and was baptized by John in the Jordan. [10] And just as he was

coming up out of the water, he saw the heavens torn apart and the Spirit descending like a dove on him. [11] And a voice came from heaven, 'You are my Son, the Beloved; with you I am well pleased.' (Mark 1:9–11)

Virtually everything we know about Jesus is packed into a short space of time – one, two or possibly three years. New Testament scholar, A.J. Levine, describes his life as follows: 'Jesus was baptized by John, debated with fellow Jews on how best to live according to God's will, engaged in healings and exorcisms, taught in parables, gathered male and female followers in Galilee, went to Jerusalem, and was crucified by Roman soldiers during the governorship of Pontius Pilate'.

E.P. Sanders, suggests we know a little more: Jesus was brought up a Jew and remained deeply Jewish all of his life. His intention was not to create a new religion but when he left Nazareth as an adult, he met the prophet John (the Baptist) and was baptised when he experienced a divine vision. This led to a ministry in Galilee where he called disciples and preached about the Kingdom of God. He became a noted healer, teacher and prophet. Around 30 CE, he travelled to Jerusalem to celebrate Passover and during the visit created a disturbance in the Temple. He had a final meal with his disciples before being arrested and interrogated by Jewish authorities, led by the high priest, before being executed by the Romans.

It is clear from even E.P. Sanders' description that there are numerous gaps in the life of Jesus and that the Gospel accounts are episodic. We do not have contemporary newspapers telling us what was going on in Galilee in 30 CE or the diaries of people who knew him. Even the Gospel of Mark was written more than three decades after the death of Jesus and what most scholars consider to be the earliest New Testament text, Paul's First Epistle to the Thessalonians, was written around 50 CE.

As a result, Christian writers have had nearly 2,000 years to fill the gaps, retell the stories and interpret the sparse accounts. They have added to the existing Gospels and even produced new Gospels not included in the New Testament such as the Gospel of Thomas (discovered in 1945 but dating back to the first century CE).

The editorial process began from very early on, partly because the practice of discipleship in the Middle East resulted in a strong oral tradition, which produced collections of his words and deeds. At first, the need to write down these reminiscences was unnecessary as the disciples expected the Kingdom of God (to be discussed in the next chapter) to arrive and Jesus to return. However, as they died, the danger arose that Jesus' story would be forgotten or, perhaps worse, told incorrectly.

In the end, we only have a general outline of Jesus' life as well as brief stories, sayings and parables, and from them we learn a lot but we still cannot write a 'history of Jesus' in the modern sense.

In order to understand how Jesus changed the world, we now consider where he preached, whom he taught and how he died.

Where did Jesus Preach?

Can anything good come out of Nazareth? (John 1:46)

Jesus went throughout Galilee, teaching in their synagogues and proclaiming the good news of the kingdom and curing every disease and every sickness among the people. (Matthew 4:23)

Palestine in Jesus' day was part of the Roman Empire. The strip of land along the Mediterranean where he preached lies at an extraordinary location. Ruled by Rome's ally, Herod the Great, King of Judea from 37–4 BCE, Palestine offered the only available land route between Asia and Africa: to the west, the Mediterranean Sea, to the east a mountainous, virtually impassable stony desert. Only two roads, one along the coast and the other along the central mountain chain, allowed a north–south passage. Whoever controlled the strip of land located between Syria and Egypt, two of Rome's most valuable possessions, controlled the major land route for trade or military activity between the great empires.

Roman imperial policy required a loyal and peaceful Palestine, which Herod achieved and was consequently given freedom to govern his kingdom as he wished – as long as the requirements of stability and loyalty were met. When he died shortly after Jesus' birth, his kingdom was divided into five parts. Herod Antipas, supported by a small Roman army, received Galilee, which became an imperial province and included the village of Nazareth. Known as 'that fox' according to Luke, he is remembered for the execution of John the Baptist and for his contemptuous treatment of Jesus.

Rural, rather than urban, Galilee provided the setting for most of Jesus' ministry. He primarily roamed the towns, villages and countryside and likely knew only one city – Jerusalem – although he would have visited Sepphoris, 5 miles from Nazareth. The Synoptic Gospels describe Jesus going to Jerusalem only in the last week of his life (unlike John's Gospel which depicts Jesus in Jerusalem from an early stage).

Although Galilee experienced some unrest (Acts 5:37 reports that Judas the Galilean caused trouble), the situation there was relatively calm in comparison with Judea, which was governed directly from Rome and was a challenging and sometimes rebellious province. Its capital was Jerusalem.

Jerusalem

A story is told about a journalist in Jerusalem who lived in a flat overlooking the Western Wall. Every day he looked out of the window and saw an old man praying vigorously. One day he introduced himself to the old man and asked, 'How many years have you prayed at the wall and what are you praying for?' The old man replied, 'I have prayed every day for twenty-five years. In the morning I pray for world peace and in the afternoon I pray for the eradication of disease'. The journalist is amazed. 'How does it make you feel to come here every day for twenty-five years and pray for these things?' he asks. The old man looks at him sadly. 'Like I'm talking to a wall'.

Jerusalem was the religious and geographical heart of Judaism. In the first century CE, it was a city of hustle and bustle, the streets crowded with people as well as donkeys, chickens, dogs and other animals. Like today, as the reader who has walked through the Old City will realise, it was dominated by narrow alleys, with enough room on the pavement for only one or two handcarts at the same time.

Houses were built two or three storeys high and the poor would live with their extended families. Lazarus, Mary and Martha, for example, lived together in Bethany near the Mount of Olives. Jesus joined them during his stay in Jerusalem. Wealthier homes contained a *mikveh* (a ritual bath) but most people used the public ritual baths. At its centre was the Temple where Jews, including Jesus, would come together to worship. Luke 2 describes how Jesus was brought as a child to be 'presented' at the Temple:

[22] When the time came for their purification according to the law of Moses, they brought him up to Jerusalem to present him to the Lord [23] (as it is written in the law of the Lord, 'Every firstborn male shall be designated as holy to the Lord'), [24] and they offered a sacrifice according to what is stated in the

law of the Lord, 'a pair of turtle-doves or two young pigeons.' (Luke 2:22–24)

The Roman prefect and his troops would also come to Jerusalem, especially during the festivals, which were sometimes occasions for civil disturbance. They stayed in the Antonia Fortress, overlooking the Temple court, so they could keep vigil.

Although Palestine was not on the edge of revolt during Jesus' lifetime, there were tensions and regular outbursts of violence, especially in the capital. Thirty years after his death there was a major rebellion (which Josephus called 'The Jewish War') and freedom movements regularly exploited the city's religious setting, as well as the large fervent crowds, in attempts to overcome Roman rule and secure Jewish sovereignty.

The Roman prefect was Pontius Pilate who used the local authorities, such as the high priest assisted by a council (called the *Sanhedrin*), to govern on a day-to-day basis. However, the Romans did not leave all matters in their hands and they did not, for example, have the right to proclaim the death penalty. During the pilgrimage festivals, in particular, the prefect took active control and Roman soldiers tried to ensure stability.

Caiaphas, the high priest, held the office from 18–36 CE, longer than anyone else during that period, indicating that he was, from the Roman point of view, reliable. Since he and Pilate were in power together for ten years, they must have established a close working relationship.

According to E.P. Sanders, the high priest had the difficult task of mediating between the remote Roman prefect and the local populace, which was hostile toward pagans and wanted to be free of foreign interference. His political responsibility was to maintain order and to see that tribute was paid.

Who did Jesus Teach?

[27] After this he went out and saw a tax-collector named Levi, sitting at the tax booth; and he said to him, 'Follow me.' [28] And he got up, left everything, and followed him.

[29] Then Levi gave a great banquet for him in his house; and there was a large crowd of tax-collectors and others sitting at the table with them. [30] The Pharisees and their scribes were complaining to his disciples, saying, 'Why do you eat and drink with tax-collectors and sinners?' [31] Jesus answered, 'Those who are well have no need of a physician, but those who are sick; [32] I have come to call not the righteous but sinners to repentance.' [33] Then they said to him, 'John's disciples like the disciples of the Pharisees, frequently fast and pray, but your disciples eat and drink.' (Luke 5:27-33)

Jesus was known for the people with whom he associated and dined. Dominic Crossan suggests that table fellowship and the places where Jesus and his followers ate are key to understanding his ministry. Many Gospel accounts depict Jesus teaching around a meal (or about food) and his table was a place of contact and conversation until his final meal, The Last Supper, which Jesus shared with his disciples during Passover.

> [22] While they were eating, he took a loaf of bread, and after blessing it he broke it, gave it to them, and said, 'Take; this is my body.' [23] Then he took a cup, and after giving thanks he gave it to them, and all of them drank from it. [24] He said to them, 'This is my blood of the covenant, which is poured out for many. [25] Truly I tell you, I will never again drink of the fruit of the vine until that day when I drink it new in the kingdom of God.' (Mark 14:22–25)

Crossan suggests that by dining with people of a different social rank, Jesus would have shocked Romans; and by dining with people from outside of Judaism, he would have shocked his fellow Jews. Most shocking to all, however (even to his disciples), was that many tax collectors and sinners ate with him (Matthew 9:10). Jesus had a concern and showed compassion for the lowly and despised that transcended the rules of the ancient world, as demonstrated by his comment to the crowds who followed him, 'What goes into a man's mouth does not make him unclean, but what comes out of his mouth, that is what makes him unclean' (Mark 7:15).

It is for this reason, I think, that Jesus attracted ordinary Jews to his teachings and to follow his ministry and possibly also some Gentiles who lived nearby. It would be a mistake, however, to think that Jesus was a hedonist. Nor, unlike John the Baptist, was he an ascetic; nor did he lead a stern life. His teachings served to feed the multitudes rather than instruct them how to go without. Jesus is even castigated for not being as serious as John the Baptist: 'The Son of Man came eating and drinking,' Jesus said, 'and they say, "Look, a glutton and a drunkard."' In other words, he was criticised for being high-spirited but this was because he was interested in Jews who lived normal and ordinary lives, rather than in the wealthy or religious elite.

With which Jews did Jesus associate most of all? Josephus describes the many ways to be Jewish in the first century and mentions four groups: Pharisees; Sadducees; Essenes; and Zealots. The Gospels never mention the Essenes, although the Dead Sea Scrolls (which originate from the Essene community) parallel some of the teachings of John the Baptist, such as the proximity of the Final Judgment, baptism and an ascetic life. Jewish zealots were active from the time of the Maccabees until the last Jewish revolt against Rome in 132–5 CE. Josephus accuses them of destroying the Temple in the war against Rome and kidnapping Jews as hostages or killing those whom they regarded as traitors. The Zealots are hardly mentioned in the New Testament although Luke (6:15) includes Simon the Zealot among the twelve disciples.

The Gospels make clear that Jesus' major dealings were with Pharisees and Sadducees. Both are mentioned as regularly arguing with Jesus and as members of the Sanhedrin that tried Paul (Acts 23:7–8). Sadducees were mainly wealthy aristocrats, were associated with worship in the Temple and collaborated with Greek and then Roman rule.

The Pharisees – other than the followers of Jesus – were the only Jewish group to survive the effects of the disastrous Jewish rebellion against Rome and the destruction of the Temple in 70 CE. They considered themselves the authentic followers of Moses and Ezra, adapting old codes for new conditions but whilst they were active in the community, they neither governed politically nor controlled public worship. Although they are prominent as the main rivals of Jesus in the Gospel accounts, they actually had more in common with Jesus than any other group. They shared many beliefs such as in the coming of the Messiah, the existence of angels, life after death, resurrection of the dead, immortality and the Day of Judgement. The harsh criticism of the Pharisees has as much to do with the rivalry between the communities in which the Gospels were written as with anything that happened during the lifetime of Jesus. It is not by chance that in the Passion Narratives, the one Jewish group that disappears from the New Testament accounts is the Pharisees. Indeed, according to Luke (13:31), the Pharisees came to warn Jesus that Herod planned to kill him.

The level of overlap and coherence between the teachings of Jesus and the Pharisees probably outweighs the areas of difference of opinion. This is demonstrated by a story about Rabbi Hillel, who lived around the time of Jesus. When a pagan came to Hillel asking if he could teach him the whole of the Torah while standing on one foot, Hillel replied, 'What is hateful to yourself, do not do to your fellow man. That is the whole Torah; the rest is just commentary. Go and study it'. (Shabbat 31a)

Likewise (but stated positively), Jesus instructed the crowds who were following him:

> [12] In everything do to others as you would have them do to you; for this is the law and the prophets. (Matthew 7:12).

And of the Pharisees, in who was Jesus most interested? As we have suggested, the tenor of Jesus' teaching was not anger – although he was angry at times – but compassion, especially towards human frailty. He worked not among the powerful but among the lowly, not to be a stern taskmaster but to offer comfort. Most of all, he called sinners and tax collectors to join his fellowship, something that offended many of his contemporaries.

Such people were not simply occasional transgressors but were viewed as brazenly breaking the commandments and living beyond Jewish practice and law. E.P. Sanders suggests that it is better to understand them as 'wicked' rather than 'sinners', which explains why Jesus' table fellowship caused such consternation. Tax collectors in particular were known for being corrupt and abusing their position of power.

It is not difficult to see how Jesus' championing of the wicked as well as the poor, and his miraculous healing of the sick would have been irritating, even threatening, to those in power. When one adds to this some ambiguous parables, which could easily be interpreted as a dramatic, sweeping call for change, irritation could easily become exasperation, particularly at the pilgrimage festival of liberation: Passover.

The End of Jesus' Ministry

After a short ministry, Jesus was picked up by the authorities in Jerusalem at Passover time. Following some kind of trial (or trials) he was executed on the charge of being a rebel leader, 'king of the Jews', perhaps in 30 or 33 CE. Like thousands of Jews in that period, he was killed by crucifixion, a horrible form of execution designed to torture the victim for as long as possible.

The events that led to Jesus' death have been vigorously debated over the centuries, and assessment of these events has fuelled hostility against Jews as 'Christ-killers'. In general, the Gospels tend to exaggerate the responsibility of the Jewish leaders in Jesus' death and to minimise the role of Pilate and the Romans. This has had a far-reaching and fateful effect on Jewish-Christian relations.

The Gospels record contradictory traditions associated with different trials and include a conviction of Jesus for blasphemy by Jews who could hardly have construed his claims as blasphemy at the time and a sentence to death by Romans who did not find him guilty of any crime against the state. He was charged with making a threat to destroy the Temple (of which he was acquitted) but his answers during cross-questioning led to another charge, that of blasphemy and of this he was finally convicted. This anyway, is how the four Gospels tell it.

And yet, in a Jewish context the claim to be 'Son of the Blessed (i.e. God) or to be the Messiah is not blasphemous. Historically, we know that there were Jews who made this claim both before and after Jesus, but no record indicating that it was considered 'blasphemous' exists. More to the point is whether the Romans would have considered his claims and actions to be a political threat.

The narrators present the Roman authority, Pilate, as being uneasy about condemning Jesus to death. This is strange because he was known as a despotic and ruthless dictator. For example, Luke mentions 'the Galileans, whose blood Pilate mingled with their sacrifice' in the Temple (13:1–4). Most Christian sources seek to excuse Pilate from responsibility for the death of Jesus, which scholars understand as an attempt to present Christianity as unthreatening to the Romans.

Whilst Jews were recognised by the Romans as members of legal *collegia* or associations and Judaism was a *religio licita* or a legal religion, as Christians came to be distinguished from Jews by the Roman authorities, they did not enjoy a similar legal status. Indeed, they were often persecuted. The difference in legal status is significant. Roman recognition of Judaism was partly based on its antiquity, whereas Christianity, because it was a new religion, was viewed suspiciously. Although the relationship between Christianity and Judaism was (and is) theologically close, it was important for the Gospel authors and early church to play down Roman concerns about the rebelliousness and trustworthiness of Christians. The accounts of the trial and the death of Jesus seek to achieve this goal.

By the time the Synoptic Gospels had been written, the Romans had crushed a Jewish revolt and destroyed the Temple. Jesus is defended from the accusation that he was personally involved in a threat to its destruction, which was an attempt to demonstrate to the Roman authorities that Jesus (and his followers) should not be associated with insurrection. The Gospels explain Jesus only predicted its destruction, e.g. Matthew 24:

> As Jesus came out of the temple and was going away, his disciples came to point out to him the buildings of the temple. [2] Then he asked them, 'You see all these, do you not? Truly I tell you, not one stone will be left here upon another; all will be thrown down'. (Matthew 24:1–2)

But according to E.P. Sanders the question of the charge about destroying the Temple should not be so easily set aside. All of the Gospels record that Jesus performed some sort of action in the Temple, representing its symbolic destruction, because he believed that afterwards the world would be radically transformed:

> [15] Then they came to Jerusalem. And he entered the temple and began to drive out those who were selling and those who were buying in the temple, and he overturned the tables of the money-changers and the seats of those who sold doves; [16] and he would not allow anyone to carry anything through the temple. [17] He was teaching and saying, 'Is it not written, "My house shall be called a house of prayer for all the nations"?'
>
> 'But you have made it a den of robbers.'
>
> [18] And when the chief priests and the scribes heard it, they kept looking for a way to kill him; for they were afraid of him, because the whole crowd was spellbound by his teaching. [19] And when evening came, Jesus and his disciples went out of the city. (Mark 11:15–19)

In the context of his expectation that the Kingdom of God would shortly arrive, contemporary Jewish leaders, particularly those associated with the Temple, would doubtless have felt threatened by his actions. Indeed, Jesus portrayed them as blind guides, leading their followers into a ditch (Luke 6:39). As we will see in the next chapter, he told stories of where pride is punctured, servants become masters and the poor become rich. These might have played well among the poor but mocking the hubris of leaders would likely have prevented him making friends in high places.

As for the Romans, it was a simple matter: had there been an offence against public order that was sufficiently serious to warrant taking punitive action? Was there any kind of threat to their political authority?

So, after a brief and relatively localised Galilean ministry, the story of Jesus appeared to have come to an end.

Yet his followers continue to experience Jesus after his death. According to Luke, he first appeared to Mary Magdalene, but she did not recognise him. Soon they proclaimed his resurrection, believing he would return again to establish the Kingdom of God on earth. As Peter said, 'God has raised this Jesus to life, and we are all witnesses of the fact' (Acts 2). They formed a community to wait for his return and sought to win others to faith in him as God's Messiah (Christ), declaring Jesus to be Lord and the Son of God.

2

The Teachings of Jesus

How Did Jesus Teach?

Parables

Jesus is famous for teaching through parables, making use of a genre familiar throughout the Jewish as well as the Mediterranean world. God was often represented as a ruler, a judge, a parent, the owner of a vineyard or field; the people of Israel were depicted as servants, children, a vine or flock; the judgment was represented as a harvest or a reckoning; and God's reign as a feast or wedding. Jesus' audience would immediately have understood these tropes and the context in which they were used.

His parables did more than reflect or describe the world in which he lived; rather, they enabled Jesus to create worlds. This is because parables are open, deliberately not accidentally, to more than one level of interpretation. When asked by his disciples why he spoke in parables (Matthew 13:10–13), Jesus explained that he sometimes deliberately cloaked them in ambiguity, which gave him the opportunity to expound on their meaning to those he taught.

Although his parables were not inevitably subversive, revolutionary interpretations, as well as his preaching, would probably have made the authorities uneasy as both implied a reversal of social and political status. The following parable illustrates:

[23] For this reason the kingdom of heaven may be compared to a king who wished to settle accounts with his slaves. [24] When he began the reckoning, one who owed him ten thousand talents was brought to him; [25] and, as he could not pay, his lord ordered him to be sold, together with his wife and children and all his possessions, and payment to be made. [26] So the slave fell on his knees before him, saying, 'Have patience with me, and I will pay you everything'. [27] And out of pity for him, the lord of that slave released him and forgave him the debt. [28] But that same slave, as he went out, came upon one of his fellow-slaves who owed him a hundred denarii; and seizing him by the throat, he said, 'Pay what you owe'. [29] Then his fellow-slave fell down and pleaded with him, 'Have patience with me, and I will pay you'. [30] But he refused; then he went and threw him into prison until he should pay the debt. [31] When his fellow-slaves saw what had happened, they were greatly distressed, and they went and reported to their lord all that had taken place. [32] Then his lord summoned him and said to him, 'You wicked slave! I forgave you all that debt because you pleaded with me. [33] Should you not have

had mercy on your fellow-slave, as I had mercy on you?' [34] And in anger his lord handed him over to be tortured until he should pay his entire debt. [35] So my heavenly Father will also do to every one of you, if you do not forgive your brother or sister from your heart. (Matthew 18:23–35)

Healing, Crowds and Disciples

Although he taught in parables, Jesus' ministry was better known for his miracles and healings. Some have viewed them as fictional and others proof that Jesus was more than a human being. Neither is helpful for understanding Jesus because whilst miracles were striking and significant, they did not indicate that the miracle worker was anything other than human. A number of Jewish contemporaries were also known for their miraculous activity such as Hanina ben Dosa, who lived in the Galilee or Honi the Circle-drawer who was known for successfully praying for rain. The need for rational explanations is a modern one.

Importantly, however, miracles were seen as accrediting a spokesperson for God and in the case of Jesus, they were also signs of the coming of the Kingdom of God. Miracles attracted crowds and added to his fame which spread throughout the Galilee, as Matthew 8 illustrates:

When Jesus had come down from the mountain, great crowds followed him; [2] and there was a leper who came to him and knelt before him, saying, 'Lord, if you choose, you can make me clean'. [3] He stretched out his hand and touched him, saying, 'I do choose. Be made clean!' Immediately his leprosy was cleansed. (Matthew 8:1–3)

He was also well known for calling disciples to follow him. It was Jewish tradition for a rabbi to attract disciples, although Jesus chose his disciples rather than disciples choosing him. Disciples might be expected to leave their family to closely follow their teacher wherever he went, so closely indeed that a rabbinic blessing was applied to followers, 'May you be covered in the dust of your rabbi'. Disciples would not simply learn the teachings of their rabbi but would act on them, to the point of imitating his life. For example, if the rabbi prayed a certain way, so did the disciples.

Although they may have been a select few, the twelve disciples were important to Jesus not only for spreading his teachings but also for facilitating his preaching to the crowds he encountered during his ministry.

Whilst appointing disciples and attracting crowds enabled Jesus to preach to large numbers of people, they were also politically dangerous, which is one reason why Herod Antipas executed John the Baptist (according to Josephus). During the lifetime of Jesus, crowds and disciples mattered very much.

Teaching with Humour

Miracles and parables, with their use of common language and commentary on everyday situations, spoke directly to ordinary people. Jesus preached with an open style and an often-overlooked feature was his use of humour. Ecclesiastes states there is, 'a time to weep and a time to laugh' (3:4) and the Psalms speak of a God who 'laughs at the wicked' (2:4; 37:13; 59:8). Yet, New Testament readers sometimes assume that because the teachings of Jesus are serious, so is the teacher. Of course, neither Old nor New Testaments consist of books of jokes but their lack of textual indicators to inform the reader of a joke, as well as no punctuation (not even exclamation marks!) mean that humour is often missed.

It should not be surprising that Jesus uses humour as Jewish comics were famous from ancient times to the modern day – from the matriarch Sarah who laughed when told she would have a son (and named Isaac for that laughter) to Woody Allen who said that 'if you want to make God laugh, tell him about your plans'.

Ordinary life in the first century CE was difficult and comic relief was welcome: comedy, especially Jewish comedy, is often about coping in difficult conditions and laughter keeps everyone going. Some psychologists have deconstructed Jewish humour in terms of managing external hostility through self-mockery, as Freud wrote, 'I do not know whether there are many other instances of a people making fun to such a degree of its own character'.

A Yiddish proverb illustrates what he meant: 'want to alleviate your big-time worries? Put on a tighter shoe.'

Humour was a means to reach a wide audience and break down barriers between ordinary people, setting them at ease and making them more receptive to the message of ministry. Note, for example, Jesus' use of comic absurdity in Matthew 23 in his critique of scribes and Pharisees:

> [23] Woe to you, scribes and Pharisees, hypocrites! For you tithe mint, dill, and cummin, and have neglected the weightier matters of the law: justice and mercy and faith. It is these you ought to have practised without neglecting the others. [24] You blind guides! You strain out a gnat but swallow a camel!

Those who heard him speak might have been shocked that he was taking on the establishment, but they would also have enjoyed his clever turns of phrase and plays on words. The comedy is even more apparent with knowledge of Aramaic, Jesus' native tongue, as the Aramaic for gnat is *galma* and the word for camel is *gamla*.

Moral instruction was intrinsic to his humour and in a warning about judging others, Jesus said, 'How dare you say to your brother, "Please, let me take that speck out of your eye", when you have a log in your own eye?' (Matthew 7:4). Rather than expounding the meaning of hypocrisy, his listeners would just have laughed at and reflected on an absurd scene.

The purpose of his wit is also demonstrated by naming Peter as the rock upon which 'I will build my church'. Firstly, Peter was anything but a rock in difficult situations (he famously pretended not to know Jesus on three occasions during the trial narratives) and secondly, an attentive reader would realise there is some of Peter in everyone. Jesus teaches, with humour, that none should take themselves too seriously.

Nathanael provides another example. Before meeting Jesus he asked, 'can anything good come from Nazareth?' but Jesus had an immediate riposte: 'Behold, an Israelite indeed, in whom is no guile!' Listeners would quickly realise that the name Jacob, the father of the Israelites whose name was changed to Israel, meant 'full of guile' or 'deceiver'. With a touch of sarcasm as well as humour, Jesus declares, 'Here is truly an Israelite in whom there is no deceit'. In other words, Jesus cleverly announces he can trust Nathanael who then becomes one of the apostles.

By welcoming Nathanael into his inner circle we see the clearest indication that as well as being a teacher, Jesus had a sense of humour.

The Kingdom of God

The Kingdom of God was the central message of the teaching of Jesus. Mark 1:14–15 introduces Jesus with these words:

Jesus came to Galilee, proclaiming the good news of God, [15] and saying, 'The time is fulfilled, and the kingdom of God has come near; repent, and believe in the good news'. (Mark 1:14–15)

The Aramaic term for kingdom, *malkut*, (in Greek, *basileia*) refers not to a geographical area but to the activity and sovereign power of a king. Unfortunately, there is little agreement about what the Kingdom of God signifies ... Is it the same as heaven? Should it be equated with the church? Perhaps, it might be understood as social reform? Or is the Kingdom of God found in the heart?

The Gospels depict Jesus as expressing all of the above, demonstrating why the concept of the Kingdom of God appeals to a wide range of Christians: those who prioritise the pursuit of justice and peace ('social reform'); those who pursue a spiritual life ('in the heart') and those who view the institutional church as the Kingdom of God on earth.

Perhaps as uncertain is whether the kingdom is already present or is to occur in the future. Jesus announces that the kingdom has come but that it also has yet to arrive. In the Lord's Prayer Jesus teaches his disciples to pray 'Your Kingdom come', and that the kingdom is in the future. The Last Supper also looks forward to that day when Jesus will drink anew in the Kingdom of God.

In other passages, however, it is equally clear that the Kingdom of God is already present. Not only had the long-awaited messianic banquet begun (Luke 14) but also the kingdom was already 'within you', according to Luke 17:

[20] Once Jesus was asked by the Pharisees when the kingdom of God was coming, and he answered, 'The kingdom of God is not coming with things that can be observed; [21] nor will they say, "Look, here it is!" or "There it is!" For, in fact, the kingdom of God is among you'.

For myself, I suggest the contradiction between 'now' and 'in the future' is an apparent one, only as the parable of the mustard seed (Matthew 13:31–3) demonstrates: the Kingdom of God is both present *and* in the future. As a mustard seed, the kingdom has entered the world virtually unnoticed but will soon be a great tree, encompassing the earth. This is because the kingdom is embodied in an insignificant band of disciples and followers who in the near future will prevail and inaugurate a new rule on earth: God's reign.

Perhaps more important than timing, is how to enter the Kingdom of God. According to Matthew 7:

[21] Not everyone who says to me, 'Lord, Lord', will enter the kingdom of heaven, but only one who does the will of my Father in heaven. (Matthew 7:21)

(Matthew regularly used the rabbinic term 'Kingdom of Heaven' rather than Kingdom of God. They are interchangeable much as the use of 'heaven' today, such as the exclamation, 'Thank Heaven!'). Like contemporary rabbinic teaching (e.g. Mishnah, Berachot 2:2), Jesus explains that the way to enter the kingdom is through living in obedience to the will of God:

> [25] Just then a lawyer stood up to test Jesus. 'Teacher,' he said, 'what must I do to inherit eternal life?' [26] He said to him, 'What is written in the law? What do you read there?' [27] He answered, 'You shall love the Lord your God with all your heart, and with all your soul, and with all your strength, and with all your mind; and your neighbour as yourself' (Deuteronomy 6:5). [28] And he said to him, 'You have given the right answer; do this, and you will live.' (Luke 10:25–8)

Time and time again, like the biblical prophets, Jesus condemns those who believed the 'right' doctrine or did the 'right' ritual but failed to do what God really desired: obey God by doing justice, loving mercy and walking humbly (Micah 6:8). In order to enter the Kingdom of God, Jesus taught it was necessary to serve the poor and oppressed, marginalised and sinful.

In the Lord's Prayer, Jesus teaches his disciples through prayer that a fundamental change in behaviour is required:

> [9] Pray then in this way:
> 'Our Father in heaven,
> hallowed be your name.
> [10] Your kingdom come.
> Your will be done,
>   on earth as it is in heaven.

[11] Give us this day our daily bread.

[12] And forgive us our debts,

as we also have forgiven our debtors.

[13] And do not bring us to the time of trial,

but rescue us from the evil one.'

[14] For if you forgive others their trespasses, your heavenly Father will also forgive you;[15] but if you do not forgive others, neither will your Father forgive your trespasses.

(Matthew 6:9–15)

The petition, 'Thy Kingdom come' (like the rabbinic prayer, the *kaddish*), glorifies God and looks towards the establishment of God's rule in the world and to a new era. For Jesus, the Kingdom of God was closely related to the imminent arrival of the End Times and a day of judgment – 'the last things' when God's reign on earth will begin and God's rule of justice and peace will be established (Isaiah 9:7). This pointed to the end of the political power of the ruling elite, a time when God would send a Messiah who would judge the worthy to 'inherit the Kingdom'. The role of judge is assigned to Jesus who will judge humans according to their deeds and the kingdom was a divine gift that could not be secured by human effort.

Regardless of whether the kingdom had actually arrived, Jesus was sure a turning point of God's plans for Israel had taken placed. Possibly, he recognised in his ministry the signs of it (see discussion of Messiah, below), but he certainly looked to the future for its arrival 'with power'. Indeed, he may well have regarded his own death as the providential condition of its full establishment and expected the final consummation in a relatively short time.

Repentance

[11] Then Jesus said, 'There was a man who had two sons. [12] The younger of them said to his father, "Father, give me the share of the property that will belong to me". So he divided his property between them. [13] A few days later the younger son gathered all he had and travelled to a distant country, and there he squandered his property in dissolute living. [14] When he had spent everything, a severe famine took place throughout that country, and he began to be in need. [15] So he went and hired himself out to one of the citizens of that country, who sent him to his fields to feed the pigs. [16] He would gladly have filled himself with the pods that the pigs were eating; and no one gave him anything. [17] But when he came to himself he said, "How many of my father's hired hands have bread enough and to spare, but here I am dying of hunger! [18] I will get up and go to my father, and I will say to him, 'Father, I have sinned against heaven and before you; [19] I am no longer worthy to be called your son; treat me like one of your hired hands.'" [20] So he set off and went to his father. But while he was still far off, his father saw him and was filled with

compassion; he ran and put his arms around him and kissed him. [21] Then the son said to him, "Father, I have sinned against heaven and before you; I am no longer worthy to be called your son". [22] But the father said to his slaves, "Quickly, bring out a robe – the best one – and put it on him; put a ring on his finger and sandals on his feet. [23] And get the fatted calf and kill it, and let us eat and celebrate; [24] for this son of mine was dead and is alive again; he was lost and is found!" And they began to celebrate'.

[25] 'Now his elder son was in the field; and when he came and approached the house, he heard music and dancing. [26] He called one of the slaves and asked what was going on. [27] He replied, "Your brother has come, and your father has killed the fatted calf, because he has got him back safe and sound." [28] Then he became angry and refused to go in. His father came out and began to plead with him. [29] But he answered his father, "Listen! For all these years I have been working like a slave for you, and I have never disobeyed your command; yet you have never given me even a young goat so that I might celebrate with my friends. [30] But when this son of yours came back, who has devoured your property with prostitutes, you killed the fatted calf for him!" [31] Then the father said to him, "Son, you are always with me, and all that is mine is yours. [32] But we had to celebrate and rejoice, because this brother of yours was dead and has come to life; he was lost and has been found."' (Luke 15:11–32)

Closely related to the announcement of the Kingdom of God is Jesus' call for repentance, which is not as easy as it sounds since simply saying 'sorry' is not a passport to repentance. Jesus follows Old Testament teaching that the penitent must be truly sorry for sin (2 Samuel 13:13), and put an end to evildoing, while beginning to do good (Psalm 24:4).

C.S. Lewis describes the act of repentance, as taught by Jesus, as follows:

> fallen man is not simply an imperfect creature who needs improvement; he is a rebel who must lay down his arms. Laying down your arms, surrendering, saying you are sorry, realising that you have been on the wrong track and getting ready to start life over again from the ground floor – that is the only way out of our 'hole'. This process of surrender – this movement full speed astern – is what Christians call repentance. Now repentance is no fun at all. It is something much harder than merely eating humble pie. It means unlearning all the self-conceit and self-will that we have been training ourselves into for thousands of years. (*Mere Christianity*)

In the parable above, Jesus depicts God as a father who welcomes home his prodigal son returning in sorrow for his misdeeds. He teaches that repentance was always possible no matter how far one had run away from God. This image is captured by the Hebrew term, *teshuvah*, (meaning 'to return') implying that repentance is a 'change of direction'. *Teshuvah* (*metanoia* in Greek) means more than 'remorse', which must precede it, but is rather a 're-turning' to God.

The returning prodigal son shows that repentance is about going home and Jesus says, 'there is rejoicing in the presence of the angels of God over one sinner who repents' (Luke 15:10). William Temple, Archbishop of Canterbury from 1942–44, commented: 'To repent is to adopt God's viewpoint in place of your own … In itself, far from being sorrowful, it is the most joyful thing in the world, because when you have done it you have adopted the viewpoint of truth itself and you are in fellowship with God'.

Jesus' teaching on repentance emphasises the mercy of God over the judgment of others. This is demonstrated by his willingness to associate with prostitutes and adulteresses, tax collectors and brigands. Jesus taught that sin was not an immovable stain but a straying from the right path and that by the effort of turning anyone can redirect his destiny. Sin separates humanity from God but repentance provides a way back.

Closely connected is the concept of forgiveness, which is also central to Jesus' teaching: 'Whenever you stand praying, forgive, if you have anything against anyone, so that your Father who is in heaven will also forgive you your transgression' (Mark 11:25). Jesus instructs his followers to forgive so that God will forgive them, as succinctly expressed by Luke: 'Do not judge, and you will not be judged. Do not condemn, and you will not be condemned. Forgive, and you will be forgiven' (Luke 6:36–7).

No one is excluded from Jesus' call for repentance. He made this clear when a group of people came to him with two pieces of bad news: Pilate had killed innocent people and others had perished when the tower of Siloam collapsed. Jesus took the occasion to warn even the bearers of the news that 'unless you repent, you will all likewise perish' (Luke 13:1–5).

Therefore, none is excluded. All need repentance. And the need is urgent. This is why his demand for repentance is central to his preaching that the Kingdom of God is near: 'The time is fulfilled, and the Kingdom of God is at hand; repent and believe in the gospel' (Mark 1:15).

Prophet-Healer-Messiah

[10] When he entered Jerusalem, the whole city was in turmoil, asking, 'Who is this?' [11] The crowds were saying, 'This is the prophet Jesus from Nazareth in Galilee'. (Matthew 21:10–11)

Jesus echoes the language and hopes of the biblical prophets, who were called by God to deliver a message. When a prophet spoke, he spoke in the name of God, believing that the divine spirit had directed his words. Likewise, Jesus speaks with the conviction that he was called by God and preaches with authority about the arrival of the Kingdom of God. Like Amos, he announces doom to the unrepentant but comforts the penitent.

At times he was polemical, using adversarial discourse and verbal combat following the rhetoric of the time (as in the Dead Sea Scrolls). When Jesus, like the biblical prophets, subjects the community to polemical exhortations, the motivation is to reform the listener. The later church, however, invoked the polemic to condemn and distorted the original text to serve different theological agendas (e.g. anti-Judaism or the condemnations of heresies) than Jesus himself.

Unlike the prophets, however, Jesus does not begin his teaching with the common phrase, 'thus says the Lord'; nor like the rabbis does he does say, 'the Torah teaches'. Rather, Jesus showed independence, speaking as one 'having authority' (Mark 1:22). Most notably, he placed himself, rather than God, in the role of forgiver of sins and Matthew 9 shows how this caused controversy:

[2] And just then some people were carrying a paralysed man lying on a bed. When Jesus saw their faith, he said to the paralytic, 'Take heart, son; your sins are forgiven.' [3] Then some of the scribes said to themselves, 'This man is blaspheming.' [4] But Jesus, perceiving their thoughts, said, 'Why do you think evil in your hearts? [5] For which is easier, to say, "Your sins are forgiven", or to say, "Stand up and walk"? [6] But so that you may know that the Son of Man has authority on earth to forgive sins' – he then said to

the paralytic – 'Stand up, take your bed and go to your home'. [7] And he stood up and went to his home. [8] When the crowds saw it, they were filled with awe, and they glorified God, who had given such authority to human beings. (Matthew 9:2–8)

The healing of the paralytic demonstrated to the crowd that Jesus had the authority to forgive sin and grant repentance. As he said earlier to his disciples, 'I want you to know that the Son of Man has authority on earth to forgive sins'. (Matthew 9:6)

The title 'Son of Man' (and the less common, 'Son of God') shed light on Jesus' self-understanding, as well as on how his followers perceived him, because it is his most popular self-designation. He used 'Son of Man' both in a generic sense ('human being') and in a self-referential sense ('I'). Having come across his preference for ambiguity before, we might justly conclude that he chose this title because of its double meaning.

Another deliberate ambiguity, in my view, concerns whether Jesus claimed to be the Messiah. Jewish messianic movements were well known in first century CE and the term Messiah is derived from the Hebrew *mashiach*, meaning 'anointed', and translated into Greek as *christos* (thus Jesus came to be known as Christ).

[13] Now when Jesus came into the district of Caesarea Philippi, he asked his disciples, 'Who do people say that the Son of Man is?' [14] And they said, 'Some say

John the Baptist, but others Elijah, and still others Jeremiah or one of the prophets'. [15] He said to them, 'But who do you say that I am?' [16] Simon Peter answered, 'You are the Christ, the Son of the living God'. [17] And Jesus answered him, 'Blessed are you, Simon son of Jonah! For flesh and blood has not revealed this to you, but my Father in heaven. [18] And I tell you, you are Peter, and on this rock I will build my church, and the gates of Hades will not prevail against it. [19] I will give you the keys of the kingdom of heaven, and whatever you bind on earth will be bound in heaven, and whatever you loose on earth will be loosed in heaven'. [20] Then he sternly ordered the disciples not to tell anyone that he was the Christ. (Matthew 16:13–20))

When Jesus is arrested in Jerusalem and brought before the high priest, he is asked, 'Are you the Messiah?' Mark records that Jesus said 'I am' (14:61), whereas according to Matthew he replied, ambiguously, 'You have said so' (26:63). In Luke's account, the whole assembly asks Jesus the question, which he refuses to answer at all by saying, enigmatically, 'If I tell you, you will not believe' (Luke 22:67).

Towards the end of his ministry Jesus did publicly claim to be the Messiah by a dramatic and choreographed entry into Jerusalem. The cries of 'hosanna' (Hebrew for 'help' or 'save now') demonstrate that the crowd viewed Jesus' entry as a king and messiah. Jesus would have realised that

such an entry would not have gone unnoticed by either
the Roman or Temple authorities.

> When they were approaching Jerusalem, at Bethphage
> and Bethany, near the Mount of Olives, he sent two
> of his disciples [2] and said to them, 'Go into the village
> ahead of you, and immediately as you enter it, you will
> find tied there a colt that has never been ridden; untie it
> and bring it. [3] If anyone says to you, "Why are you doing
> this?" just say this, "The Lord needs it and will send it
> back here immediately."' [4] They went away and found a
> colt tied near a door, outside in the street. As they were
> untying it, [5] some of the bystanders said to them, 'What
> are you doing, untying the colt?' [6] They told them what
> Jesus had said; and they allowed them to take it. [7] Then
> they brought the colt to Jesus and threw their cloaks on
> it; and he sat on it. [8] Many people spread their cloaks
> on the road, and others spread leafy branches that they
> had cut in the fields. [9] Then those who went ahead and
> those who followed were shouting,
> 'Hosanna!
> 'Blessed is the one who comes in the name of the
> Lord!
> [10] 'Blessed is the coming kingdom of our ancestor
> David!
> 'Hosanna in the highest heaven!' (Mark 11:1–10)

In biblical times, the kings sometimes (rightly)
viewed prophets as a threat to their rule but the term

messiah was not applied to any. Another feature, which differentiated Jesus from the prophets, is that he routinely called God, 'Father' and Matthew very often has him say, 'My father'. His public affirmation of a close and personal relationship with God is a distinguishing feature. Although God was called 'Father' by many of his contemporaries (and still is, by billions of people in many of the world's religions), it seems likely that Jesus' designation of God as Abba ('daddy' in Aramaic) was particularly characteristic of him. Abba is mentioned only twice in the rabbinic literature.

Moreover, as we saw in the Lord's Prayer, Jesus also encouraged his followers to call God 'Father'. Two references to Abba in Paul's Epistles suggest that this form was used, possibly liturgically, from very early times. For example, Galatians 4 indicates that Paul interpreted Jesus's divine sonship as crucial:

[4] But when the fullness of time had come, God sent his Son, born of a woman, born under the law, [5] in order to redeem those who were under the law, so that we might receive adoption as children. [6] And because you are children, God has sent the Spirit of his Son into our hearts, crying, 'Abba! Father!' (Galatians 4:4–6)

Paul's teaching that humans become children of God because Jesus was his son is not so far from the Synoptic authors' emphasis that Jesus knew God as (his) father, and encouraged his followers to share in that relationship.

However, by turning to Paul, we are now moving to the post-Easter Christian experience of Jesus, reflecting Paul's own interpretations as much as the views of other early Christians. We have now completed our exploration of Jesus in History and move onto considering the Jesus of History.

3

The Development and Diversity of Christianity

Although the preceding chapters have showed that we are limited in our knowledge of the historical Jesus, the religion named after him has become the largest in the world with 2.2 billion adherents today. For a man who seemed to have brought about little change in the world during his lifetime, is it possible to identify anyone who inspired more after his death?

All four Gospels conclude with the death and resurrection of Jesus, which are the climax of their accounts. By his death Jesus inspired change and through their experience of his resurrection, his followers changed the world.

This was brought home to me when I recently attended an Anglican baptism and heard the following words, based on the Nicene Creed, spoken by baby Elizabeth's parents and godparents:

I believe in Jesus Christ, his only Son, our Lord who was conceived by the Holy Spirit, born of the Virgin Mary, suffered under Pontius Pilate, was crucified, died and was buried; he descended to the dead. On the third day, he rose again; he ascended into heaven, he is seated at the right hand of the Father; and he will come to judge the living and the dead.

Clearly, belief in the resurrection and the future return of Jesus Christ are central to Christian belief. His final appearance is reported as being forty days after the resurrection when he was 'carried up' into heaven where he sits on the right hand of God (Mark 16).

The resurrection heralded a new era in the history of the world and is marked by the celebration of Easter, which takes place around the same time as Passover and the Last Supper is understood as a Passover meal. Jesus gave Passover a new meaning when he identified the bread (probably *matzah*, unleavened bread) as his body and the cup of wine as his blood. Both Easter and Passover symbolise the redemptive activity of God and demonstrate a continuing close association between Christianity and Judaism. Even the name of Easter in Greek and Latin is *Pascha*, a transliteration of the Aramaic for Passover. (In English, the festival borrowed its name from a pre-Christian Celtic goddess of the spring, Eostre.)

What was it about Jesus that Christians sought to change the world in his name? Part of the answer is that Christians believe that Jesus was not just a character *in* history but also someone who is alive in the present and will play a crucial role in the future. This I describe as the Jesus *of* history who is called the Son of God, the Son of Man, the Messiah (Christ), the Word (logos) by whom the world was created, the Passover sacrifice, the Suffering Servant who takes on the sins of the world, not to mention the new high priest.

Jesus remains the source and focus of Christian belief today and his presence nourishes Christians.

The Birth of Christianity

The Early Centuries

In my 'Introduction to Christianity' class, I begin by telling students that the first Christians were Jews. But this seemingly simple assertion is a lot more complicated than it looks, since the term 'Christian' came into parlance towards the end of the first century. They were all Jews certainly, but were they also 'Christians'?

In terms of history, Christianity did not begin with Jesus. As we have already noted, Jesus was born, lived and died a Jew. Surely a founder of a new religion is supposed to belong to the new religion? Yet the Gospels depict Jesus as a Jew who taught among fellow Jews. Even the Romans who executed him, inscribed the cross upon which he was crucified the words, 'King of the Jews'.

Most scholars believe that the term 'Christian' is first used in the second century CE and it is mentioned only three times in the New Testament, starting in Antioch where 'the disciples were called Christians' (Acts 11:26).

If Christianity did not begin with the historical Jesus, does it begin fifty days after the resurrection with Pentecost, which marks the descent of the Holy Spirit on the apostles and is the traditional date for the establishment of the church?

> [2] And suddenly from heaven there came a sound like the rush of a violent wind, and it filled the entire house where they were sitting. [3] Divided tongues, as of fire, appeared among them, and a tongue rested on each of them. [4] All of them were filled with the Holy Spirit and began to speak in other languages, as the Spirit gave them ability. (Acts 2:2–4)

Yet, Jesus' followers continued to observe Jewish practice for some decades afterwards, most notably by worshipping in the Temple. Indeed, the last words of Luke's Gospel states they 'were continually in the Temple blessing God', demonstrating that 'Christians' were still perceived as Jewish by other Jews. Even during the war against the Romans in 66–70 CE, about thirty years after the crucifixion, Josephus describes Jesus' followers as being involved in an internal Jewish conflict.

Perhaps Christianity began with Paul (Saul) of Tarsus who died around 67 CE? However, like Jesus, Paul saw himself as a Jew all of his life and although his writings are clearly Christ-centred, he never abandoned Judaism, describing himself as 'a Pharisee, son of a Pharisee' (Acts 23:6). Whilst the drama of his 'Damascus Road experience' and vision of the risen Jesus have led some scholars to the conclusion that he left one religion (Judaism) and joined another (Christianity), Paul did not convert; rather, he preached that God had revealed Himself in a new way, through the death and resurrection of Jesus. As he said in his last letter, 'I myself am an Israelite, a descendant of Abraham, a member of the tribe of Benjamin' (Romans 11:1).

In my view, the first sign of Christianity occurs when Gentiles join the community where 'there is neither Jew nor Greek; there is neither slave nor free, there is neither male nor female' as Paul wrote in Galatians (3:28). Something new emerges, a crossing of boundaries, which binds Jews and non-Jews in a new entity, in which they meet as equals. The self-understanding of the Jewish adherents was, of course, still that of Jews who had found their Messiah. But what of the Gentiles? Although they also believed in the one God of Abraham, Isaac and Jacob and also in Jesus, they did not become Jewish. This community of Jewish and Gentile followers of Jesus marks a step towards separation of the two religions, but a separation that had not yet occurred. There were numerous partings along the way.

We know this because Paul repeatedly visited synagogues alongside his non-Jewish mission. Although he increasingly reached out to Gentiles, he did not want them to follow Jewish practice (such as circumcision and the dietary laws). This led to the Apostolic Council in Jerusalem, which, according to Paul at least, recognised that the non-Jewish world was called to the God of Israel without having to be incorporated into the people of Israel.

Paul was instrumental to the development of Christianity because he was a Roman citizen and took advantage of the extensive system of Roman roads. He went on numerous missionary journeys throughout the Roman Empire and established churches, after which he would write letters of counsel and encouragement. Most scholars think at least seven of these letters became part of the New Testament (although more are ascribed Paul but were probably written by his disciples).

The environment in which he travelled was already rich with religious diversity, including not only Judaism but also the political religion of the Roman state, the personal religion of the mystery cults and the intellectual and ethical schools of Greek philosophy. Whilst the immediate religious context of Christianity was Judaism, the pagan religions and philosophies were also highly significant. Roman state cults adopted the Eastern pattern of deifying emperors and honouring the gods of individual cities. The cult of the emperor, which began with Augustus, was used primarily to reinforce and test political loyalty. Many Christians (and Jews) refused to offer a sacrifice in honour of Caesar and were persecuted for it.

The pagan mystery religions were also influential but their characteristics are not well known due to their secretive nature and the lack of surviving writings. Most held in common not only secrecy but the adoption of syncretistic belief and practice, and a focus on the death and resurrection of a saviour-god.

As Christianity expanded, it also came into contact with Greek philosophy. Hellenistic thinking became significant and most of the early church fathers were Greek-speaking Gentiles, trained in classical philosophy. Like Hellenistic Jews, they believed classical philosophy to be compatible with religious teachings.

Early Christianity also put into practice the compassion shown by Jesus by establishing hospitals, a kind of health service and social services – everything from soup kitchens to money for the poor. Christians also established mutual social support for those who joined the church. Thus, the growth of Christianity was not only due to its religious message but also the result of social action and the establishment of welfare institutions, serving the church and wider society.

Christians also tried to accommodate existing norms by, for example, adapting pre-existing holidays and festivals. Christmas, for example, was originally part of the great festival of the Winter Solstice. With its good digestion system Christianity appropriated some pagan traditions making it familiar as well as attractive to Gentiles.

At the same time, especially in the second and third centuries, Christians faced persecution from outside the church and doctrinal division from within. Christian leaders, the church fathers, wrote defences against false claims made about Jesus and against other Christians from outside the church, as well as polemics opposing false teachings spreading within the church. Doctrines were developed and solidified, the canon of the New Testament was formed and the notion of 'apostolic succession', starting with Peter, established a system of authority.

This was also a time of Roman persecution, perhaps partly because worship of Jesus Christ, crucified under Pontius Pilate, a Roman governor, was perceived as an affront and threat to the social order. In 250 CE, Emperor Decius decreed that everyone had to sacrifice to the Roman gods and many Christians refused, leading to a great number of martyrdoms. However, it was too late to crush Christianity, which had already become a significant proportion of the Roman population. Christianity, like Judaism, had learned how to survive and (eventually) overcome oppression.

A major turning point in Christian history came in the fourth century. Under the Emperor Diocletian the Roman Empire was split into two (East and West) but within a few years, Constantine reunited the empire after he defeated Maxentius in 312 CE. He ascribed his victory to a vision of the cross, experienced the night before battle. This marked his conversion to Christianity (although he was only baptised on his deathbed in 337). One of Constantine's first acts after his victory was to issue the Edict of Milan, a toleration of all religions. Persecution of Christianity ceased and thousands now found it straightforward to convert.

Under Constantine, the Roman Empire took over the institutions of the church and a sense of stability returned.

He wanted to replace Rome as capital and looked for a new city. He chose Byzantium in the East, as it was strategically located on the European side of the Bosporus, controlling the route to and from the Black Sea, providing an excellent harbour that was easily defended. Constantine repaired the city's walls, built churches and, in the spirit of Roman tolerance, allowed new pagan temples (although pagan sacrifices were forbidden). After his death, the city was renamed Constantinople (and today is called Istanbul).

Constantine's mother Helena also became a devout Christian and made a pilgrimage to the Holy Land, following the path taken by Jesus and identifying key places from his ministry. She built shrines and churches such as the Church of the Nativity at Bethlehem and the Church of the Holy Sepulchre in Jerusalem. Thanks to Helena, Christianity has as many holy sites in modern day Israel, Palestine and Jordan as do Jews (and to a lesser extent, Muslims). Indeed, she was perhaps as instrumental as Paul in the development of Christianity because from then onward, pilgrimage to the Holy Land became an aspiration for all Christians. According to the Israeli Tourism Ministry, for example, over 1.6 million Christians visit Israel each year (nearly twice as many as the number of Jewish tourists), many of whom follow the path laid down by Helena in their desire to walk in the footsteps of Jesus.

Constantine hoped Christianity would help heal a divided empire, but divisions remained and in 325 CE he faced a theological dispute (Arianism) that threatened fracture. The issue was whether Jesus Christ was more than a human but less than God. He called a council at Nicaea so that bishops could resolve these differences. They condemned Arianism and declared the Son (Jesus Christ) to be of 'one substance' with the Father (God). This was later called the Nicene Creed and, as the Anglican baptism liturgy demonstrates, is still proclaimed today, providing a mainstream theological definition of what it means to be a Christian.

By the time Constantine died in 337, Christianity had established itself as the religion of the Roman Empire. Until he had become emperor, Jesus' followers could and did live as Jews or as Gentiles and there was a co-existence. His rule marks the moment in history when Christianity finally and completely parted from Judaism. We can conclude, therefore, that the birth of Christianity took place over centuries, rather than decades after the life, death and resurrection of Jesus Christ.

From Constantine to the Modern Era

Over the next few centuries, allied with the Roman Empire (and its successor the Holy Roman Empire), Christianity grew in power until it became the Christendom that encompassed the entire western world in the Middle Ages and Renaissance. Its contribution to civilisation and culture also grew significantly during this time: Christian scholars preserved literacy in Western Europe; Christian architects designed great cathedrals, which remain today among the most iconic feats of architecture; and many of Europe's greatest universities were founded by the church, based on the template of the monastery.

However, religious, cultural, and political differences between the Eastern and Western churches remained strong. Religiously, they had different views on the use of icons, the nature of the Holy Spirit, and when Easter should be celebrated. Culturally, the Greek East tended to be more philosophical and abstract in its thinking, while the Latin West, tended toward a more pragmatic and legal-minded approach.

Constantinople assumed pre-eminence in the East, becoming the main rival to Rome, because other Eastern bishoprics such as Alexandria and Antioch had succumbed to Muslim rule by 650 CE. However, it faced theological disputes with other eastern churches, thus strengthening the political position of the bishops of Rome (as the Popes are called), who made increasing claims of authority. Matters came to a head in 1054, when Pope Leo IX excommunicated the patriarch of Constantinople, who condemned the Pope and excommunicated him in return. Known as the Great Schism, the church has been officially divided ever since.

There had been mutual excommunications before, but they had not resulted in a permanent schism. The year 1054 was a watershed in church history and the mutual excommunications were not lifted until 1965, after Pope Paul VI and Patriarch Athenagoras met in Jerusalem (where else?) the previous year. However, the schism has never been healed.

In the 1400s, some western Christians began to publicly challenge the institutional church, speaking out against corruption and the abuse of authority. They called for a return to the gospel teachings, rejecting traditions such as purgatory, the cult of the saints and relics, and the practice of withholding the communion wine from non-clergy. They also began to translate the Bible – then available only in Latin – into native languages but did not have much success, and most were executed.

However, in 1517, a German monk named Martin Luther posted his 95 Theses, which included the decrying of the practice of selling indulgences, on his church door. Promoting the doctrine of justification by faith alone, he shared many of the ideas of those early reformers. A sense of growing German nationhood and the invention of the printing press ensured that Luther had greater protection than his predecessors and his teachings spread quickly.

As the Reformation developed in Germany, various groups in other parts of Europe also began to break away from the Catholic Church. Reformed Christianity developed in Switzerland based on the teachings of Ulrich Zwingli and John Calvin. When it spread to Scotland under John Knox, the reformed faith became Presbyterianism. Switzerland was also the birthplace of the Anabaptists, spiritual ancestors of today's Quakers and Baptists. Anglicanism was established in 1534 when King Henry VIII broke from the authority of the Pope.

In the seventeenth century, Christians embarked on the journey across the Atlantic, to the promise of religious freedom and economic prosperity in the New World. Quakers came to Pennsylvania, Catholics to Maryland, and Dutch Reformed to New York, writing monumental theological tracts along the way, including John Locke's 'A Letter Concerning Toleration' (1689). Later came Swedish Lutherans and French Huguenots, English Baptists and Scottish Presbyterians. The church not only inspired countless theological, philosophical and political writings but also deeply influenced music and the arts. Christian artists like Michelangelo and Raphael produced some of the most celebrated works of art. Similarly, Christian composers like Bach, Handel, Beethoven and Schubert are among the most admired classical composers.

The period from about 1648 to 1800 was an age in which reason (as opposed to revelation and dogma) became increasingly important, but so did religious revival movements that attracted the masses. John Wesley was a revivalist preacher who founded a small group of preachers and bible students who focused on holy living and social action. They came to be known as Methodists.

Evangelical revivals led to the growth of missionary activity, demonstrated by Jonathan Edwards, a leader of the First Great Awakening in North America and the Wesley brothers, John and Charles. In previous centuries, missionary activity had almost exclusively been Roman Catholic in origin and tied with trade. For example, in 1493, Pope Alexander VI instructed the Spanish navy to spread Christianity as well as engage in commercial activity.

British-led missionary activity also expanded, especially after India was incorporated into the British Empire. In 1806 Henry Martyn arrived in India and translated the New Testament into Urdu. There were also many missionaries in Africa, best known was David Livingstone and in 1857 his *Missionary Travels and Researches in South Africa* was published. In 1860 the first World Missionary Conference was held in Liverpool and the motto of the 1910 Edinburgh conference was apt, 'the evangelisation of the world in this generation'.

Christian Denominations

Christianity has three major branches, normally called denominations. Each has its own distinctive beliefs or practices, but is generally considered a denomination of Christianity if core doctrines like the divinity of Jesus Christ and the authority of the Bible are accepted. Relationships between denominations range from mutual respect and co-operation to denial that the other group is really Christian. The three are: Roman Catholicism, Orthodoxy and Protestantism. Some regard Anglicanism as a fourth branch that fits none of these categories, while others categorise it as Protestant.

Roman Catholicism represents the continuation of the historical church as it developed in Western Europe, and is led by the bishop of Rome (known as the Pope and the 'first among equals'). Distinctive Catholic beliefs include the doctrines of transubstantiation and purgatory, and practices include devotion to the saints and Mary, and use of the rosary.

Orthodoxy (which includes the Greek, Russian, Serb, Ukrainian and several other mainly eastern churches) is the continuation of the historical church as it developed in Eastern Europe and Asia Minor. It does not make allegiance to the Pope, emphasises the use of icons in worship and has its own dating of Easter. Other cultural, political, and religious differences exist as well.

Protestants also do not acknowledge the authority of the Pope, reject many Catholic traditions and beliefs, emphasise the importance of reading the Bible and most hold to the doctrine of salvation by faith. Protestantism encompasses numerous groups (sometimes and confusingly also called denominations), including Lutherans, Baptists, Methodists, Presbyterians, Pentecostals and Evangelicals (and possibly also Episcopalians or Anglicans).

Those who remained Roman Catholic after the Reformation argued that central regulation of doctrine is necessary to prevent confusion and division within the church and corruption of its beliefs. Those reformers who broke from the church, on the other hand, insisted that it was precisely this policy of control that had already led to corruption of the true faith. They demanded that believers be allowed to read the Scriptures for themselves and act in accordance with their conscience. This issue of religious authority continues to be a fundamental difference in perspective between Catholic and Orthodox Christians on one hand, and Protestants on the other.

Today, 51 per cent of the world's 2.2 billion Christians are Catholic. Protestants make up 37 per cent and Orthodox Christians comprise 12 per cent.

Christianity Today

Distribution of Christian Population by Region

Americas	804,070,000
Europe	565,560,000
Sub-Saharan Africa	516,470,000
Asia Pacific	285,120,000
Middle East / North Africa	12,480,000

Source: Pew Research Center's Forum on Religion & Public Life, Global Christianity, December 2011

Christians are geographically widespread, representing a third of the estimated global population of 6.9 billion (based on 2010 figures). Their number has grown from 600 million in 1910 to 2.2 billion in 2010 (but the world's overall population has risen equally rapidly, meaning that Christians make up about the same portion of the world's population today as they did a century ago – 32 per cent).

This apparent stability, however, masks a momentous shift. A century ago, about two-thirds of the world's Christians lived in Europe but today only about a quarter of all Christians are European. At the same time, Christianity has grown enormously in sub-Saharan Africa and the Asia-Pacific region. The Christian proportion of the population in sub-Saharan Africa climbed from 9 per cent in 1910 to 63 per cent in 2010, while in the Asia-Pacific region it grew from 3 per cent to 7 per cent.

Christianity today has developed far beyond the Galilean ministry of Jesus:

- Less than 1 per cent of the world's Christians are found in the Middle East-North Africa, the smallest number of Christians of any region (13 million and declining);
- Indonesia, a Muslim-majority country, is home to more Christians than all the countries in the Middle East-North Africa region combined;
- Nigeria has more than twice as many Protestants as Germany, the birthplace of the Reformation;
- Brazil has more than twice as many Roman Catholics as Italy;
- Christians form a majority of the population in 158 countries (two-thirds of all countries in the world)

(Source: Pew Research Centre on Religion and Public Life)

The Global South and the Global North

A century ago, the Global North (defined as North America, Europe, Australia, Japan and New Zealand) contained more than four times as many Christians as the Global South (the rest of the world) but by 2010 more than 1.3 billion Christians lived in the Global South (61 per cent), compared with 860 million in the Global North (39 per cent).

But even though Christians are more numerous in the Global South, the concentration of Christians is much higher in the Global North, where 69 per cent of the population is Christian. By contrast, 24 per cent of the people living in the Global South are Christian. This reflects the fact that the total population of the Global South is about 4.5 times greater than the population of the Global North.

Another way of looking at the distribution of Christians around the world is by region. Numerically, Europe no longer dominates. Rather, both the largest number and the highest proportion of Christians live in the Americas. More than a third of Christians worldwide live there and nearly nine-in-ten people are Christian. The three largest Christian populations (USA, Brazil and Mexico) account for 24 per cent of all Christians, about the same as the whole of Europe (26 per cent) and all of sub-Saharan Africa (24 per cent).

10 Countries in the Americas with the Largest Number
of Christians

Countries	Estimated 2010 Christian Population	Percentage of Population that is Christian	Percentage of World Christian Population
United States	246,780,000	79.5%	11.3%
Brazil	175,770,000	90.2%	8.0%
Mexico	107,780,000	95.0%	5.0%
Colombia	42,810,000	92.5%	2.0%
Argentina	34,420,000	85.2%	1.6%
Peru	27,800,000	95.6%	1.3%
Venezuela	25,890,000	89.3%	1.2%
Canada	23,430,000	68.9%	1.1%
Chile	15,310,000	89.5%	0.7%
Guatemala	13,700,000	95.2%	0.6%
Subtotal for the 10 countries	*713,690,000*	*86.1%*	*32.7%*
Total for Rest of Region	*90,380,000*	*8.7%*	*4.1%*
Total for region	*804,070,000*	*86.0%*	*36.8%*
World Total	***2,184,060,000***	***31.7%***	***100%***

Population estimates are rounded to the ten thousands.
Percentages are calculated from unrounded numbers. Figures
may not add exactly due to rounding.

Source: Pew Research Center's Forum on Religion & Public Life,
Global Christianity, December 2011

Sub-Saharan Africa and the Asia-Pacific region have a combined population of about 800 million Christians and five of the top ten countries with the largest Christian populations are either in Africa (Nigeria, Democratic Republic of the Congo and Ethiopia) or Asia (Philippines and China). The fastest growth is in sub-Saharan Africa (from 9 million in 1910 to more than 516 million in 2010) and in the Asia-Pacific region (from 28 million in 1910 to more than 285 million in 2010) (Source: Pew Research Centre on Religion and Public Life).

Finally, a Pew Forum study issued in 2015, projecting the future of world religions to 2050, makes interesting reading for European Christianity, as Europe is the only region projected to see a decline in its total population between 2010 (745 million) and 2050 (700 million) and a decline in the numbers of Christians. Although they will continue to be the largest religious group in the region, Europe's Christian population is expected to drop by about 100 million people, falling from 553 million in 2010 to 454 million in 2050.

The remaining religious groups in Europe are projected to grow in number due to a combination of higher fertility, younger populations and net gains via migration and conversion. Europe's Muslim population is projected to increase by 65 per cent, growing from 43 million in 2010 to 71 million in 2050, but the largest group will be the religiously unaffiliated population which is expected to grow by about 16 per cent, from 140 million in 2010 to 162 million in 2050.

China

We end this chapter with a consideration of Christianity in China as it brings us back to the discussion of the origins of Christianity in the Roman Empire. Although Christianity arrived in China in the seventh century CE, 300 years after Constantine, it is only in the last two decades that it has substantially flourished, during a time of great social and economic change.

When the Communists took over the country in 1949, there were less than 4 million Christians (in a population of 540 million). China's Communist leaders, like the Romans two millennia earlier, viewed Christianity with deep unease but like them found it hard to control. Persecution of Christians and destruction of 'illegal' churches failed to stem growth. The Communist Party, as Constantine did, is seeking new ways to respond, especially as Christianity seems to have penetrated the government's own ranks.

Today, official figures state that China has 23 million Christians but scholars estimate the number is much more – perhaps as many as 100 million (with 7–10 per cent annual growth). It is startling to note that China now has more Christians than members of the Chinese Community Party (87 million). Most are evangelical Protestants. On current trends there will be 250 million Christians by 2030, making China's Christian population the largest in the world. This speed of growth is similar to that in fourth-century Rome, when Christianity became the religion of the Roman Empire.

Having failed to control Christianity through more forceful means, *The Economist* noted in 2015, the Communist Party is now engaging with it more constructively: 'There has been an upsurge in religion with new churches and temples springing up everywhere.' Christianity's traditional association with a foreign (i.e. Western) culture and its perceived threat to the social order (like the banned Falun Gong movement) worries party officials less than previously. Their concern is with stability rather than religion and it is noteworthy that Christianity is especially popular at the Chinese universities – where the future members of the country's Communist Party study.

Even the more awkward situation of the Roman Catholic Church – allegiance to Rome is easily seen as a sign of treachery – has improved. In 2015, the first Catholic bishop for some years was consecrated, approved by both the Chinese government and the Vatican.

Finally, the Communist Party needs the help of religious believers to deliver social services, and Christian (and Buddhist) groups are willing and able to help, persuading the party leadership that Christians are not seeking to overthrow it.

It is too soon to know what the consequences will be but I would hazard a guess that the influence of China on the development of Christianity will be as great as any in world history since the conversion of Constantine and the Roman Empire 1,700 years ago.

4

Jesus from the Perspective of Other Faiths

Jewish perspectives

[37] The two disciples heard him say this, and they followed Jesus. [38] When Jesus turned and saw them following, he said to them, 'What are you looking for?' They said to him, 'Rabbi' [which translated means 'teacher'], 'where are you staying?' (John 1:37-8)

There are three proofs that Jesus was Jewish:
1. He went into his father's business
2. He lived at home until he was 30
3. He was sure his mother was a virgin, and his mother was sure he was God.
(Jewish joke book)

The words and deeds of Jesus the Jew, called rabbi on fifteen separate occasions in the New Testament, have been, and are, an inspiration to countless millions of men and women. He was a child of Jewish parents, brought up in a Jewish home and raised in accordance with Jewish tradition. Throughout his life, Jesus lived among Jews and his followers were Jews. No other Jew in history has rivalled Jesus in the magnitude of his influence. Is it not strange that most Jews have given such little attention to the life and teaching of this outstanding Jew?

Yet, this is true because the Christian followers of Jesus came to cherish beliefs about his life, which Jews could not hold. When the church persecuted Jews in an effort to convert them, Jewish indifference to Jesus turned to hostility. For centuries it was very hard for any Jew even to think of Jesus without difficulty. Up until recently, most Jews have chosen not to think of him at all.

Yet, in the last few decades in particular, there has been a dramatic change in Jewish attitudes towards Jesus. A re-evaluation has been taking place, initially as we have seen, by Christians but also more recently by Jews, re-awakening to the Jewish context of his life and ministry. This is a significant shift from the norm, which was for Jews to look for defects in the New Testament or for parallels in rabbinic writings. 'What was true could not be new and what was new could not be true' was a phrase that summarised many Jewish views of the teachings of Jesus. Jews today take a much more balanced approach.

When Jesus responded to the question 'what commandment is the first of all', he answered as any Jew would (then or now) with the *Shema*, a Jewish declaration of faith, which is recited at every Jewish service, day and night (Deuteronomy 6:4–9), followed by the famous command of Leviticus about love of neighbour (19:18), which is also a fundamental precept of Judaism.

[28] One of the scribes came near and heard them disputing with one another, and seeing that he answered them well, he asked him, 'Which commandment is the first of all?'[29] Jesus answered, 'The first is, "Hear, O Israel: the Lord our God, the Lord is one;[30] you shall love the Lord your God with all your heart, and with all your soul, and with all your mind, and with all your strength."[31] The second is this, "You shall love your neighbour as yourself." There is no other commandment greater than these'. (Mark 12:28–31)

Even the claim that Jesus is the Messiah is not uncommon in Judaism. Several Jews have claimed to be the Messiah and Messianic expectation is a sign of religious vitality. Simon Bar Kochba in 132 CE and Shabbetai Zvi in 1665 CE are two examples and more recently, many followers of Menachem Schneerson, known as the Lubavitcher Rebbe, considered him the Messiah. Even today, after his death in 1994 in New York, some Lubavitch Jews await his messianic return.

The main differences between Judaism and Christianity concern the belief that Jesus is God Incarnate, the Son of God the Father. Jews believe that all share the divine spirit and are stamped with the divine image and no person, not even the greatest, can possess the perfection of God.

Another difference concerns claims about his death and resurrection. For Christians, Jesus' death is the supreme example of self-sacrifice; the willing sacrifice of the Son of

God that the world might be redeemed from sin. For Jews, the significance of Jesus must be in his life rather than his death; in his teaching rather than in doctrine; in the holiness of his life rather than in the sanctity of belief.

The closeness between Jesus and Judaism explains the success of Jewish scholarship in significantly influencing New Testament studies in general and studies of Jesus in particular. Most well known is Geza Vermes who in *Jesus the Jew* (1973) opened the eyes of many to the Jewishness of Jesus, whom he depicted as a Galilean Hasid, a pious and holy man. For Vermes, Jesus was a charismatic teacher, healer and prophet. He compares him to his contemporary, Hanina ben Dosa, also a leader and healer.

More recently Amy-Jill Levine described Jesus as 'a good Jew' who taught Jews in a Jewish land. Jesus dressed, ate, taught and prayed like a Jew, argued like a Jew with other Jews, and amassed Jewish followers. Levine is also concerned to respond to some anti-Jewish interpretations which attempt to depict Jesus as unique and Jews as obsessively rule-following, unconcerned with the poor and oppressive to women. However, she also encourages Jews to appreciate Jesus in continuity with other leaders and prophets of Israel, and her co-edited, *Jewish Annotated New Testament* (2011) is not only written entirely by Jews but is intended, in part at least, for Jewish readers.

Perhaps most controversial is the work of Talmudic scholar, Daniel Boyarin, who argues that Jesus was embraced by many Jews because his messianic teachings were in line with Jewish beliefs. He suggests that the

Messianic role as understood by Jesus was an already-existing Jewish expectation that Jesus sought to fulfil and that Christology was not created for Jesus but merely applied to Jesus.

Jesus in Islam

Say (O Muslims): We believe in God and that which is revealed unto us and that which was revealed unto Abraham, and Ishmael, and Isaac, and Jacob, and the tribes, and that which Moses and Jesus received, and that which the prophets received from their Lord. We make no distinction between any of them, and unto Him we have surrendered. And if they believe in the like of that which ye believe, then are they rightly guided. But if they turn away, then are they in schism, and God will suffice thee against them. He is the Hearer, the Knower. (Sura 2:136–7)

Since Muslims and Christians make up well over half of the world's population and are, it could be argued, intertwined globally more than ever before, Muslim attitudes to Jesus are worth taking very seriously. Unsurprisingly, they demonstrate both divergence and commonality with Christian interpretations.

Like Christianity, Islam emphasises love of one God and love of the neighbour, which as we have already noted, are central also to the teachings of Jesus. For example, Muhammad is reported in the Hadith as saying, 'None of you has faith until you love for your neighbour what you love for yourself.'

Jesus is greatly honoured in Islam and described as a prophet. He appears in fifteen chapters and ninety-three verses of the Qur'an, with many descriptions similar to the New Testament accounts. For example, the Qur'an relates that Jesus was born to a virgin called Mary, preached God's word, gathered disciples, performed miracles of healing and ascended to God. He is also called the Word of God, a spirit from the divine and Muslims have interpreted Qur'anic passages to mean that Jesus will return to the earth at the end of time as *al-Masih*, the Messiah.

However, there are also problems from a Christian perspective in the portrait of Jesus (and other biblical figures such as Mary) in both the Qur'an and later Muslim Tradition. Divergences about Jesus arise in a respectful way as well as with a polemical edge. Occasionally, Christians would not recognise Qur'anic depictions. For example, although Jesus is described as being condemned to death by crucifixion he was saved through divine intervention, ascending to heaven without dying.

Another crucial difference is that for Muslims, Jesus is emphatically not the Son of God, viewed as created and not divine. The Qur'an denies any equality with God. The Jesus of the Qur'an has none of the characteristics of the Christian understanding of Son of God, and most importantly since he did not die, there is no atoning death. Thus:

They have certainly disbelieved who say, 'Allah is the Christ, the son of Mary' while the Messiah has said, 'O Children of Israel, worship Allah, my Lord and your Lord.' Indeed, he who associates others with Allah – Allah has forbidden him Paradise, and his refuge is the Fire. And there are not for the wrongdoers any helpers. They have certainly disbelieved who say, 'Allah is the third of three.' And there is no god except one God. And if they do not desist from what they are saying, there will surely afflict the disbelievers among them a painful punishment. (Surah 5:72–3)

There is of course dissent within Islam, for example, those Muslims who depict Jesus as a prophet and Messiah would not necessarily agree with the Sufi mystical notion that he is 'the seal of the saints' (proposed by Ibn al-Arabi, 1165–1240). We should remember also that Christians too, argue over Jesus' role in the plan of God's salvation.

However, because the Qu'ran and the Hadith are inspired by God, it is not easy for Muslims to recognise that their sources about Jesus might themselves be polemical, rather than an objective portrait. A similar challenge for Christians (and Jews) is the idea that the Gospels (and Torah) are believed to have been distorted by their recipients, so that they contain extraneous human material that pollutes the original unsullied divine revelation.

Interestingly, there are a number of theological similarities between Muslims and Jews in their approaches to Jesus. For example, for Muslims the belief that Jesus is God or the Son of God is defined as *shirk*, which means associating partners with God, and is therefore a rejection of God's divine oneness (*tawhid*). *Shirk* is similar to the Jewish concept of *shittuf*, which also refers to the 'association' of an additional power with God and is considered a contamination of absolute monotheism. Most importantly, both Judaism and Islam reject the possibility of the divinity of Christ.

Jesus Among Hindus and Buddhists

'Christ' is another way of saying Krsta and Krsta is another way of pronouncing Krishna, the name of God … the general name of the Supreme Personality of Godhead, whose specific name is Krishna. Therefore whether you call God 'Christ', 'Krsta', or 'Krishna', ultimately you are addressing the same Supreme Personality of Godhead … God has millions of names, and because there is no difference between God's name and Himself, each one of these names has the same potency as God. (Swami Prabhupada (1896–1977), founder of the Hare Krishna Consciousness Movement)

As surprising as it may seem, it is not unusual to see pictures of Jesus alongside Hindu gods and goddesses in

Hindu homes. In some ways, Hindus do not really see Jesus as a Christian at all and many include him alongside their own vision of Divine reality. This is because for Hindus belief is not as significant as practice, which in Sanskrit is called *sadhana*.

It is more common for a Hindu to ask, 'What is your *sadhana*?' than, 'What do you believe?' Jesus is understood by Hindus to be a *Sadhu*, a holy man, even a saint, who preached a universal message of love of God and love of humanity. He is also called an *acharya*, 'one who teaches by example' and for Hindus, Jesus' message is no different from that preached by, for example, Krishna.

One aspect of Hinduism that has an extraordinary resonance with Christianity is the concept of an *avatar*, the 'downcoming' of a god in human or animal form for the sake of humans in need. Avatar applies to any distinguished person and is understood as a manifestation of divinity. Of course, for Christians, the revelation of God in Christ is more than a 'downcoming' because Jesus is understood as the only human incarnation of God.

Nevertheless, the concept of avatar for Hindu-Christian relations means that the one God becomes, if not the many, then a plurality, (even though Hindus regard Christian Trinitarian theology as limited since for them, the nature of transcendence is a kind of divine lavishness, an overflowing in myriad forms in this world). However, Judaism and Islam seem by comparison with Christianity, to be austere in their belief in the One God.

The 'practical atheism' of Buddhism represents a different set of issues for perceptions of Jesus. Christians (and Jews and Muslims) are deeply aware of the presence of a personal, creator God who loves his creation and cares for what he has created. Yet Buddhism does not share this belief in a creator God.

When Gautama Siddhartha became the Buddha (the 'awakened one'), and woke up to life's meaning, he saw it as human liberation into the truth of things, which required individuals to sort out their own lives and liberation, with his discovery as their beacon and their guide. The fact that the gods are powerless to help, indeed, that they are dependent upon the Buddha's insight, is a far cry from Jesus' perception of a heavenly father of grace.

Yet, the Buddha is reported as offering similar teachings to Jesus such as the Buddha's comment to 'consider others as yourself' (Dhammapada 10:1), which parallels the Golden Rule. Another example is the comment by Jesus that, 'just as you did not do it to one of the least of these, you did not do it to me' (Matthew 25:45), which echoes the Buddha's command, 'if you do not tend to one another, then who is there to tend you? Whoever would tend me, he should tend the sick' (Vinaya, Mahavagga 8:26.3).

However, some Buddhists insist that Jesus was completely mistaken and have engaged in anti-Christian polemic, possibly the legacy of Western (Christian) imperialism in Buddhist lands, where Jesus was associated with missionaries who deprecated the Buddha and Buddhist culture. For example, the nineteenth-century

Japanese Buddhist scholar Inoue Enryō remarked once: 'It is neither because I favour Sakya-muni [Gautama the Buddha] nor because I am prejudiced against Jesus that I uphold Buddhism and reject Christianity. It is simply because I love truth and hate untruth.'

The Vietnamese Buddhist monk, Thich Nhat Hanh, offers a more irenic interpretation of Jesus, bringing Jesus and the Buddha together. He refers to the Buddhist story about a mother, Kisa Gotami whose baby son is dying and visits the Buddha to ask him to heal her child. The Buddha responds to her distress, by asking her to bring him a mustard seed from a house where no one has ever died. Eventually, Kisa Gotami is comforted when, unable to fulfil his request, she realises she is not alone in suffering – death and bereavement are inevitable facts of human existence.

Thich Nhat Han points out that Jesus teaches in a similar way, demonstrated by the crowd who had gathered ready to stone to death a woman accused of adultery. When Jesus asked anyone who is without sin to hurl the first stone, one by one they all turned away, having realised that everyone is a sinner.

Jesus, Communism and Liberation Movements

[16] Then someone came to him and said, 'Teacher, what good deed must I do to have eternal life?' [17] And he said to him, 'Why do you ask me about what is good? There is only one who is good. If you wish to enter into life, keep the commandments'. [18] He said to him, 'Which ones?' And Jesus said, 'You shall not murder; You shall not commit adultery; You shall not steal; You shall not bear false witness; [19] Honour your father and mother; also, You shall love your neighbour as yourself'. [20] The young man said to him, 'I have kept all these; what do I still lack?' [21] Jesus said to him, 'If you wish to be perfect, go, sell your possessions, and give the money to the poor, and you will have treasure in heaven; then come, follow me'. [22] When the young man heard this word, he went away grieving, for he had many possessions.

[23] Then Jesus said to his disciples, 'Truly I tell you, it will be hard for a rich person to enter the kingdom of heaven. [24] Again I tell you, it is easier for a camel to go through the eye of a needle than for someone who is rich to enter the kingdom of God'. (Matthew 19:16–24)

The well-known celebrity atheist, Richard Dawkins described Jesus as a great moral teacher, suggesting that, 'somebody as intelligent as Jesus would have been an atheist if he had known what we know today'. This section explores the intriguing and perhaps unexpected relationship between Jesus and communism, most of whose adherents are atheists.

Left-wing radicals sometimes exhibit a tendency to promote their radical political ideology in a manner, which is more akin to radical political theology. The influence of Christianity can be seen among those who argue that Jesus espoused communism as the ideal social system. It is this reason, it is suggested, that Jesus said that 'No one can serve two masters, for either he will hate the one and love the other, or he will be devoted to the one and despise the other. You cannot serve God and money'. (Matthew 6:24)

Of course, mainstream Marxist communists are generally atheist but Christian communists share the same conclusions, if not the underlying atheist premises. They refer to Acts 2 and 4 as evidence that the first Christians lived in a communist society and cite other biblical passages, which they believe demonstrate that communism is a natural outcome of Jesus' teaching about the Kingdom of God on earth. Thus, for a rich man to enter the kingdom he must cease to be rich.

Christian liberation theologians (as well as Christian communists in general) emphasise another aspect of the teachings of Jesus – the liberation of the poor from captivity and oppression:

[16] When he came to Nazareth, where he had been brought up, he went to the synagogue on the sabbath day, as was his custom. He stood up to read, [17] and the scroll of the prophet Isaiah was given to him. He unrolled the scroll and found the place where it was written:

[18] The Spirit of the Lord is upon me,
because he has anointed me
to bring good news to the poor.
He has sent me to proclaim release to the captives
and recovery of sight to the blind,
to let the oppressed go free,
[19] to proclaim the year of the Lord's favour.
(Luke 4:16–19)

Liberation theology is a practical example of a radical movement that grew up as a response to poverty and oppression. According to the Roman Catholic theologian, Leonardo Boff, 'If Jesus Christ were on Earth today, he would be a Marxist revolutionary.'

Liberationists argue that, following the example of Jesus, Christians should act to bring about radical social change, and the church should ally itself with the working class to do so. Some priests not only became involved in politics and trade unions but also aligned themselves with violent revolutionary movements. One of the most high profile clerics was the Archbishop of San Salvador, Óscar Romero, an outspoken advocate for the poor. He was assassinated while saying mass in San Salvador in 1980 and has been declared a martyr by Pope Francis. In 2015 he was beatified and the canonisation process continues at the time of writing.

Although Pope John Paul II opposed the actions of liberation theologians in the 1980s, Pope Francis is less concerned, perhaps partly because of his experience as leader of the Catholic Church in Argentina. In 2014, he declared that all people, even atheists, could be redeemed. 'Just do good,' he said, 'and we'll find a meeting point', echoing the word of James 2:24 that 'a person is justified by works and not by faith alone'.

Of course, the 'catch', whether atheist communists like it or not, is that from a Christian perspective their salvation is accomplished through Jesus who offered himself as a sacrifice for everyone, a 'ransom for all' (First Letter to Timothy). There is then no escape from the influence of Jesus and his teachings, regardless of a person's political leanings.

Jesus, Capitalism and Material Success

[14] For it is as if a man, going on a journey, summoned his slaves and entrusted his property to them; [15] to one he gave five talents, to another two, to another one, to each according to his ability. Then he went away. [16] The one who had received the five talents went off

at once and traded with them, and made five more talents. [17] In the same way, the one who had the two talents made two more talents. [18] But the one who had received the one talent went off and dug a hole in the ground and hid his master's money. [19] After a long time the master of those slaves came and settled accounts with them. [20] Then the one who had received the five talents came forward, bringing five more talents, saying, 'Master, you handed over to me five talents; see, I have made five more talents.' [21] His master said to him, 'Well done, good and trustworthy slave; you have been trustworthy in a few things, I will put you in charge of many things; enter into the joy of your master.' [22] And the one with the two talents also came forward, saying, 'Master, you handed over to me two talents; see, I have made two more talents'. [23] His master said to him, 'Well done, good and trustworthy slave; you have been trustworthy in a few things, I will put you in charge of many things; enter into the joy of your master'. [24] Then the one who had received the one talent also came forward, saying, 'Master, I knew that you were a harsh man, reaping where you did not sow, and gathering where you did not scatter seed; [25] so I was afraid, and I went and hid your talent in the ground. Here you have what is yours'. [26] But his master replied, 'You wicked and lazy slave! You knew, did you, that I reap where I did not sow, and gather where I did not scatter? [27] Then you ought to have invested my money with the bankers, and on my return I would have received what was my own with interest. [28] So take the talent from him, and give it to the one with the ten talents. [29] For to all those who have, more will be given, and they will have an abundance; but from those who have nothing, even what they have will be taken away. [30] As for this worthless slave, throw him into the outer darkness, where there will be weeping and gnashing of teeth'. (Matthew 25:14–30)

It is easy to see how the Parable of the Talents could be understood as depicting Jesus as a model capitalist. He uses making more money as a metaphor for making the most of life's opportunities. The man who traded with investment capital and earned profits is praised by his master (who represents God) and is rewarded by being given greater authority as well as keeping his wealth. Striking too is the criticism Jesus addresses to the man who was afraid to invest the one talent of gold entrusted to him.

Some successful Christian businessmen and women understand this to mean that Jesus endorsed the building up of wealth, earning interest and making a profit. He understood financial and material incentives. Although he never specifically commended capitalism, neither did he condemn the principle of commerce; rather the abuse of the market generated his anger. In other words, Christian capitalists would argue, Jesus condemned the corruption of capitalism, rather than capitalism itself. They might also refer to what has become know as 'the Protestant work ethic', famously outlined by Max Weber, who argued in 1905 that Protestant Christianity was an important force behind the emergence of capitalism.

In conclusion, we can see that whilst it is not possible for a Christian to be both a capitalist and a communist, Jesus' teachings can be understood as supporting both. And this apparent contradiction provides us with a clue as to how Jesus changed the world: humans can be one thing or another but Jesus can be more.

Taken further, this chapter has showed that Jesus can be praised as a rabbi by Jews and as a prophet by Muslims; as an avatar by Hindus and a holy teacher by Buddhists; a champion of the poor by revolutionaries and a model capitalist by entrepreneurs. It is the diverse applicability of his teachings, as well as the malleability of the figure of Jesus, that enables me to claim him as the person who changed the world more than any other.

And is there another way to justify such a claim? Simply this: there are more followers of Jesus than any other religion (or secular ideology) in the world.

Maps

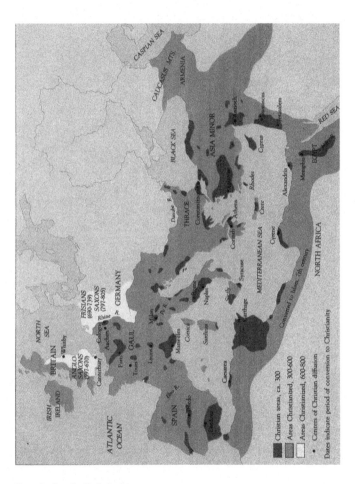

Growth of early Christianity

First-century Palestine

Glossary

Prepared by Jack Branford

Apostle
Literally meaning the 'one who is sent', such as an ambassador who represents their country. In the New Testament, the term usually refers to either Jesus' inner circle of followers but Paul also refers to himself and others who have seen the risen Jesus in person as 'apostles'

Apostolic Succession
Refers to an uninterrupted transfer of spiritual authority from the apostles through successive popes and bishops

Arianism
The belief first attributed to Arius (c.AD 250–336) that although Jesus Christ is the Son of God, he is created by God the Father and is therefore both distinct and subordinate to the Father. Arianism contradicts Trinitarian Christian orthodoxy agreed at the Council of Nicaea in 325 and was decreed a heresy

Baptism
Literally the 'plunging' of people into water. John the Baptist used baptism as a ritual to mark repentance. John baptised Jesus, and his followers in turn baptised others.

After his death, Jesus' followers adopted baptism as a sign of admission into the Christian community, associating the ritual with the death and resurrection of Jesus himself

Blasphemy
Acts of insulting or contemptuous behaviour directed towards God(s) or something else regarded as sacred

Dead Sea Scrolls
A collection of texts found in the 1947 at Qumran (near the Dead Sea), many of which are contemporary to the lifetime of Jesus and were originally part of the library of a monastic group, probably the Essenes. They include the earliest known copies of the Hebrew Scriptures as well as other documents that shed light on the Judaism of Jesus' day

Denomination
A subgroup within a religion that operates under a common name, tradition, and identity. For example, Christian denominations include: the Greek Orthodox Church, Roman Catholicism and Anglicanism

Disciple
A common name for a follower of Jesus; the term means 'pupil' or 'apprentice'

Doctrine
A belief or set of beliefs held and taught by a religion, church, or other group

Evangelical
A movement within Protestant Christianity which tends to stress: the doctrine of salvation by faith; the centrality of conversion for receiving salvation; belief in the authority of the Bible as God's revelation to humanity and evangelism

Gentile
Literally meaning 'belonging to a clan or tribe' and is commonly used in the New Testament to refer to a non-Jewish person

Hadith
Translated as 'report', 'narrative' or 'account,' hadith are collections of reports or traditions which claim to quote the prophet Muhammad

Icon
A flat panel painting (literally 'image') depicting Jesus Christ, Mary, the saints or angels. Icons are especially venerated by Orthodox Christians

Justification
A theological term, which refers to the action of being made righteous, just or free from sin in the eyes of God

Kingdom of God
Also known, especially in Matthew, as the Kingdom of Heaven, does not refer to a geographical area but to the activity and sovereign power of God or king. It is a flexible

concept and in the Gospels Jesus is depicted as equating the kingdom with: heaven, the church, social reform and the inclination of the heart. Moreover, Jesus announces that the kingdom has come in the present but that it also has yet to arrive. The Kingdom of God is thus, both present and in the future; now and not yet

Krishna
One of the most widely revered Gods across the many traditions of Hinduism. In most Hindu traditions Krishna is recognised as the eighth avatar of the Supreme God Vishnu or even as the Supreme God himself

Last Supper
The final meal that Jesus shared with his disciples before the crucifixion. The Last Supper also provides a scriptural basis for the Eucharist, also known as the Mass or Holy Communion

Liberation Theology
A radical movement originating in South America, which argues that the church should ally itself with the working class to bring about radical social change

Messiah (Christ)
Derived from the Hebrew meaning 'anointed one', refers to a prophet, priest or king. Jesus was associated with all three in the New Testament. In Greek, 'Messiah' is translated as *Christos* (thus 'Christ' in English). In Judaism,

the term applied to the expectation that God would send his anointed, a king, the heir of King David

Monotheism
The belief in a single all-powerful God. Judaism, Christianity and Islam are all monotheistic religions

Pharisees
A Jewish group following in the tradition of Moses and Ezra, adapted old laws for new situations. Contemporary with Jesus, they neither governed politically nor controlled public worship but were the only Jewish group (apart from Christians) to survive the effects of the Jewish rebellion against Rome and the destruction of the Temple in 70 CE

Purgatory
A Roman Catholic Church doctrine, which states that there is an intermediate state after physical death in which those destined for heaven must undergo purification of their sins before they can enter heaven

Repentance
A 'change of direction' and involves remorse regarding sinful actions, and a subsequent 'returning' to God and the doing of good deeds

Rosary
A form of prayer, used commonly in Catholic churches, and named after the string of prayer beads that is used to count the constituent prayers

Sabbath
A day of rest and worship and the first divine biblical command, which according to Jewish tradition, runs from Friday to Saturday evening

Sadducees
Contemporaries of Jesus, Sadducees were mainly wealthy aristocrats who were associated with worship and sacrifices in the Temple and collaborated with the Romans

Sanhedrin
Meaning 'sitting together' in an assembly and refers to the Jewish council and legislative body

Synoptic Gospels
Consist of Matthew, Mark and Luke because of their many similarities, including many of the same stories, often with similar wording and in a similar sequence

Tithe
Literally means 'a one-tenth part of something' that is given away to religious and/or charitable causes

Torah
An 'instruction' or 'teaching' and refers to both the first five books of the Bible and, according to rabbinic tradition, also of interpretations handed down and redacted in rabbinic writings, especially in the Talmud and Midrash

Transubstantiation
A Roman Catholic teaching on the Eucharist, which refers to the change of the bread and the wine into the actual body and blood of Jesus

Timeline

c. 4 BCE	Birth of Jesus
c. 26–30 CE	Ministry of John the Baptist
c. 29	Jesus begins his public ministry
c. 33	Crucifixion and death of Jesus
c. 33	Pentecost (Acts 2)
c. 35–36	Saul of Tarsus, comes to believe in Jesus as the Messiah and subsequently becomes the Apostle Paul
c. 48 CE	Council of Jerusalem (Acts 15), which decided that Gentile Christians were no longer obliged to keep many Jewish laws such as circumcision of males and food laws
c. 50–65	Paul writes various letters to Christian communities around the Mediterranean that now make up the oldest parts of the New Testament
c. 60–65	Death of Paul
c. 60–68	Deaths of the apostles Peter and James (the brother of Jesus and leader of the Church in Jerusalem)
c. 68–100	Gospel's of Mark, Matthew and Luke (Luke–Acts) are written
70	Fall of Jerusalem and destruction of the Temple

from 70	Centre of Christianity moves from Jerusalem to Antioch, Alexandria and Rome
c. **90–110**	Gospel of John and the Book of Revelation are written
c. **90–190**	Gospel of Thomas and other non-canonical Gospels are written
c. **94**	Josephus writes *Antiquities of the Jews*
from 100	Early church fathers (such as Justin Martyr, Clement of Alexandria, Tertullian and Origen) develop and defend Christian theology
249–251	First major persecution of Christians under Emperor Decius
257–260	Persecution resumes under Emperor Valerian but ends when Gallienus becomes Emperor
303	Persecution begins under Diocletian
312	Battle of the Milvian Bridge when Emperor Constantine first adopts Jesus Christ
313	Constantine issues the Edict of Milan granting Christians full rights to worship in the Roman Empire and restitution of property confiscated during the Diocletian persecution
324	Constantine moves the eastern capital of the empire to Byzantium, which is renamed Constantinople

325	Council of Nicea attempts to resolve theological differences within the church. It is agreed that Jesus was both fully human and fully divine
327	Death of Constantine
381	Ecumenical Council at Constantinople revises the Nicene Creed
***c.* 382**	Saint Jerome begins a translation of the Bible into Latin
397	Synod at Carthage agrees on the twenty-seven books that make up the New Testament canon
451	Ecumenical council at Chalcedon affirms Christ's 'Hypostatic Union' of two distinct natures united in one person
589	Insertion of the *filoque* ('and the son') clause into the Nicene–Constantinopolitan Creed at the council in Toledo
597	Augustine becomes the First Archbishop of Canterbury
787	Ecumenical council at Nicea affirms the use of icons in prayer and worship
988	Conversion of Prince Vladimir of Kiev prompts the growth of Christianity in Russia
1054	Great Schism – eastern and western churches separate
1095–1204	Crusades, which resulted in the killings of thousands of Jews (Rhineland Massacres) by Crusaders on their way to liberate the Holy Land

1216–23	Papacy grants its seal of approval to two new mendicant religious orders, the Dominicans and the Franciscans
c. **1380**	John Wycliffe translates parts of the Bible into English
1453	Constantinople falls to the Ottoman Empire
1493	Pope Alexander VI instructs the Spanish navy to spread Christianity in South America
1517	Martin Luther posts his 95 Theses in Wittenburg, Germany, beginning the protestant reformation
1526	William Tyndale publishes the first full translation of the New Testament in English.
1534	Ignatius of Loyola founds the Jesuit Order
1534	Church of England is created as the Act of Supremacy is passed and Henry VIII becomes the supreme head of the English Church
1545–63	Council of Trent – described as the embodiment of the counter-reformation by the Roman Catholic Church
1611	Publication of the King James Bible
From 1620	Christians begin to emigrate in large numbers from Europe to North America
1730–60	Protestant revival movement known as the 'Great Awakening' takes place in the USA
1738	John Wesley begins the Methodist movement

1806	Henry Martyn arrives in India and translates the New Testament into Urdu
1857	David Livingstone's *Missionary Travels and Researches in South Africa* is published
1860	First World Missionary Conference is held in Liverpool
1870–71	First Vatican council takes place affirming the doctrine of Papal infallibility
1906	Azusa Street Revival in Los Angeles starts the Pentecostal movement
1918	American evangelist Billy Graham is born
1948	World Council of Churches is founded
1962–65	Second Vatican Council takes place, beginning major reforms in the Roman Catholic Church, including transforming the relationship with Judaism
1964–65	Relations improve between the Roman Catholic and Orthodox Churches as the mutual excommunication is lifted for the first time since the Great Schism
1991	Bartholomew I is installed as the Ecumenical Patriarch of Constantinople
2000	Pope John Paul presides over a liturgy of repentance, the basis for the prayer he placed in the Western Wall in Jerusalem during his pilgrimage to Israel
2013	Pope Francis elected Pope
2013	Installation of Justin Welby as Archbishop of Canterbury

Further Reading

Abdel Haleem, M.A.S. (trans.), *The Qur'an: An English Translation* (Oxford University Press, 2008)

Barker, Gregory, *Jesus in the World's Faiths: Leading Thinkers from Five Religions Reflect on His Meaning* (Orbis, 2008)

Barrett, C.K., *The New Testament Background: Selected Documents* (SPCK, 1956)

Bauckham, Richard, *Jesus: A Very Short Introduction* (Oxford University Press, 2011)

Berger, Peter; Davie, Grace & Fokas, Effie, *Religious America, Secular Europe? A Theme and Variations* (Ashgate, 2008)

Bockmuehl, Markus (ed.), *The Cambridge Companion to Jesus* (Cambridge University Press, 2001)

Boyarin, Daniel, *The Jewish Gospels: The Story of the Jewish Christ* (The New Press, 2013)

Buckner, Richard, *The Joy of Jesus: Humour in the Gospels* (Canterbury Press, 1994)

Burkett, Delbert (ed.), *The Blackwell Companion to Jesus* (Wiley-Blackwell, 2013)

Court, John & Kathleen, *The New Testament World* (Cambridge University Press, 1990)

Crossan, John Dominic, *The Historical Jesus: The Life of a Mediterranean Jewish Peasant* (Harper, 1991)

Freedman, H. (trans.), *Hebrew-English Edition of the Babylonian Talmud: Tractate Shabbath* (Soncino Press, 1972)

Jenkins, Philip, *The Next Christendom: The Coming of Global Christianity* (Oxford University Press, 2011)

Johnson, Luke Timothy, *The Writings of the New Testament* (SCM, 1999)

Josephus, Flavius, *Jewish antiquities* (Harvard University Press, 2014)

Levine, Amy-Jill & Brettler, Marc. Z, *The Jewish Annotated New Testament, New Revised Standard Version* (Oxford University Press, 2011)

Levine, Amy-Jill, *The Misunderstood Jew: The Church and the Scandal of the Jewish Jesus* (Harper One, 2006)

Lewis, C.S., *Mere Christianity* (William Collins, 2012)

MacCulloch, Diarmaid, *A History of Christianity: The First Three Thousand Years* (Penguin, 2010)

McGrath, Alistair, *Christian Theology: An Introduction* (Wiley-Blackwell, 2010)

Moule, C.F.D., *The Birth of the New Testament* (A&C Black, 3rd ed., 1981)

Parrinder, Geoffrey, *Jesus in the Qur'an* (Oneworld, 1995)

Pelikan, Jaroslav, *Jesus through the Centuries* (Yale University Press, 1985)

Philips, Elizabeth, *Political Theology: A Guide for the Perplexed* (T&T Clark, 2012)

Sanders, E.P. *Jesus and Judaism* (Fortress Press, 1985)

Sanders, E.P. *The Historical Figure of Jesus* (Allen Lane, 1993)

The Holy Bible, New Revised Standard Version, Anglicized Edition (Oxford University Press, 1990)

Throckmorton Jr., Burton, H. (ed.), *Gospel Parallels: A Comparison of the Synoptic Gospels: New Revised Standard Version* (Thomas Nelson, 1992)

Tuckett, Christopher, *Reading the New Testament* (SPCK, 1987)

Vermes, Geza (trans.), *The Dead Sea Scrolls in English* (Sheffield Academic Press, 1995)

Vermes, Geza, *Jesus the Jew: A Historians Reading of the Gospels* (Fortress Press, 1973)

Wright, N.T. & Borg, Markus, *The Meaning of Jesus* (SPCK, 1999)

Web Links

www.catholic-resources.org/Bible/index.html
The website of Dr Felix Just of the Loyola Institute for Spirituality contains a variety of excellent materials relating to biblical studies

www.ntgateway.com
An excellent web directory of internet resources on the New Testament by Dr Mark Goodacre of Duke University

www.pbs.org/wgbh/pages/frontline/shows/religion/
Useful summaries on the historical Jesus from the website related to the American documentary *From Jesus to Christ*

www.virtualreligion.net/iho/
A website exploring the world in which Jesus lived by means of newly translated primary texts and other material

www.textweek.com/mtlk/jesus.htm
A useful guide to what is available on the web on the Gospels

http://www.ccjr.us/dialogika-resources
A useful guide to key documents and studies in Jewish-Christian relations

www.jewishchristianlit.com//Topics/JewishJesus/
A website with information on Jesus from Josephus and other Jewish sources

www.clas-pages.uncc.edu/james-tabor/
A website including a variety of essays, pictures and pieces of information on Judaism in the first Century, the New Testament and Christian origins

Acknowledgements

Writing an introductory work on Jesus is not an easy task. That it has turned out to be so rewarding is due to a significant number of people.

I would like to thank the series editor, Tony Morris, who kept me focused on the task in hand, commented on the manuscript with sensitivity and showed patience throughout. I am also grateful to Sophie Bradshaw at The History Press.

There are a number of other friends and colleagues without whose help this book would not have been completed. I would like to express thanks to my colleagues at the Woolf Institute: Sughra Ahmed, Gorazd Andrejč, Jan-Jonathan Bock, Shana Cohen, Claire Curran, Sami Everett, John Fahy, Christina Fuhr, Emma Harris, John Lyon, Alice Sandham, Tina Steiner, Matthew Teather and Esther-Miriam Wagner.

I would like to acknowledge the support of other colleagues who have been kind enough to offer constructive comments, particularly Phil Cunningham and John Pawlikowski, who read the manuscript at an early stage and offered wise advice.

I would also like to acknowledge the contributions of Peter West, who carefully read and made suggestions on the first draft, and Jack Branford who reviewed the heavily revised second draft (thank you, Tony) and produced the timeline, glossary, maps and recommended reading.

My fellow trustees have always encouraged me to write as well as to direct the Woolf Institute and I am pleased to thank them all – Waqar Ahmad, Ian Blair, Trixie Brenninkmeijer, Martin Forward, Bob Glatter, Peter Halban Khalid Hameed, Richard, Harries, David Leibowitz, Julius Lipner, Martin Paisner, Shabir Randeree, Ed Williams and Marguerite Woolf.

Finally, I would like to acknowledge the support of my family, particularly my wife Trisha and our children, Shoshana, Asher and Eliana who correctly remind me that the priorities of my life begin at home.

I dedicate this book to my father, whose love, encouragement and support are a model to all fathers. He gave me the greatest gift anyone could: he believed in me.

pocket GIANTS

A series about people who changed the world –
and why they matter.

Series Editor – Tony Morris

www.thehistorypress.co.uk